THE PRINTER'S COMPOSITION MATRIX

OAK KNOLL SERIES
ON
THE HISTORY OF THE BOOK

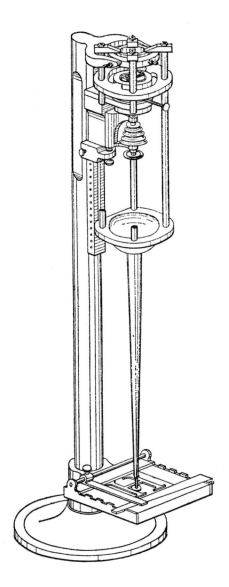

Original Benton punch-cutting machine;
from patent specification, 1885

THE PRINTER'S COMPOSITION MATRIX

A History of
Its Origin and Development

By Richard E Huss

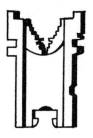

OAK KNOLL BOOKS
NEW CASTLE, DELAWARE
1985

Library of Congress Cataloging in Publication Data

Huss, Richard E.
    The printer's composition matrix.

    Bibliography: p. 53
    Includes index.
        1. Type-setting—History.   2. Type-setting machines—
History.   3. Printing, Practical—History.
4.   Typefounding matrices—History.   I. Title.
Z253.H88   1985   686.2′25   85–25914
ISBN 0–938768–09–3

CONTENTS

INTRODUCTION

This treatise discusses the development and use of the letterpress printer's *composition matrix*, showing its early multifarious forms in a way that never before has been described. It elucidates details not revealed either by the early makers of matrix-composing machines, or by the historical texts which rehearsed the development of composing machines made during the years 1885 to 1915. For the non-printer the term *composing machine* means any form of mechanical device designed to set, or compose, printers' types, as opposed to setting them by hand.

Present-day printers who are still using matrix-composing machines—usually referred to as *hot-metal typesetters*—are familiar with their matrices, but they are not familiar with their predecessors, or with the history of those problems which beset the early prototypes. The purpose of this book is to reveal some of those problems and to describe the matrices and their manipulations in many kinds of early successful matrix-composers, as well as to include for historical reasons a number of *proposed*, but never commercially produced machines, for which there are patent or other authentic records.

It will be helpful at the outset for the lay reader to know the meaning of the term *letterpress printing* (since it is now largely superceded by electronic techniques), for it is the fundamental key to understanding the process of printing from metal types. *Letterpress* signifies printing done from a relief printing-surface, like that produced by the subjects of this text, that is, the matrices used to machine-cast individual types, or sluglines. Letterpresses all work on the simple principle of transferring printing ink *directly* from the type surface to the paper.

In the 1960s this kind of composing equipment began to decline when letterpress printing gradually gave way to the inroads of computer-composition systems for offset printing. Modern printing technology uses computers for the photographic and digital composition of *letter images* (not types), with the aid of cameras and cathode ray tubes (CRT), and laser devices. Flat (planographic) plates are then produced and mounted on offset presses. These presses print indirectly, that is, the image is first printed on a rubber-dressed cylinder and is then transferred to the paper, hence the term *offset*. This method is based on Alois Senefelder's 1796 discovery of the antipathy between water and grease, resulting in the invention of lithographic printing from stone. The exposed printing areas of the offset plates—as on the stones—receive the ink and the unexposed areas receive a film of water, which has the effect of preventing the greasy ink from spreading over the entire surface of the plate. Commercial *rotary offset printing on paper* dates from 1904 when it was first exploited by Ira Rubel. Recent technology, however, through the use of electronics and computers, has technically and economically upset the balance between the two dominant methods of composition for printing—in favor of offset.

Here indeed has been a repetition of history. Just as in the earlier late-nineteenth century when the matrix systems were supplanting a centuries-old hand-set method, now *letter images* and the camera have virtually replaced the relief types cast from machine-set matrices. Yet this is not entirely true, for there are still some printers who hold—at least in part—to hot-metal composition. But their counterparts in the offset industry know nothing of a Linotype matrix or of the Linotype machine, unless they are of the older generation of printers and compositors. And it is likely that there are still many former "type-setters" (people) who operated Monotype keyboards, as well as the "cast-ermen" who produced the actual types on the separate Monotype casting machines.

So effective has this transition been, created by time and the new computer/photographic techniques, that hot-metal systems have with increasing frequency found their way to the junkyard or museum collections. But *lead is not yet dead* and for this history of matrix-composing methods it is important to bear in mind that they have led the printing industry into highly automated methods for doing rapid composition of reading matter.

During the late nineteenth century a surprisingly large number of attempts were made to create both patrix-using machines and matrix-using machines in which the "cold" and the "hot" concepts were considered as substitutes for the time-honored method of setting types by hand. All the patrix (cold) ideas were abortive or failures, while the matrix (hot) machines had some early successes and proved to be headed in the right direction for machine composition.

Both the patrix and matrix classes are of equal age, dating from Joseph Mazzini's "Uniplane" system of 1843 which was intended to use both patrices and *disposable* matrices. Up to the year 1885, in which this synopsis starts, there were at least 23 United States patents on patrix methods alone, preceding the matrix methods.

Although the matrix classes were extremely diversified in construction and operation, they all followed one fundamental principle, that of assembling or moving matrices and casting either single-types, or sluglines, which is the theme of this treatise.

Two appendices following the text of this book list chronologically a total of 166 patented inventions, most of them of American origin. If the name of a machine is known, it is included with the date, the inventor's name, and a reference to the source material.

Due to the technical nature of this work it is difficult to cast *every* term in simple layman's language, so brief explanations are given at scattered points to aid the reader in understanding the terms.

Bibliographically there is no such a thing as a literature on this subject. Perhaps this treatise will fill the gap.

(x)

THE PRINTER'S COMPOSITION MATRIX

MATRIX =

The copper mould with a punch struck in by which type is cast. Also called "strikes." Charles T. Jacobi, *The Printer's Vocabulary*. London: The Chiswick Press, 1888.

That part of a mould in which types are cast, which contains a representation of the letter to be made. J. Luther Ringwalt, *American Encyclopaedia of Printing*. Philadelphia: Menamin & Ringwalt, 1891.

The sunken molds in which type is cast, produced by an impression from a punch. It is also the mold made from a page of type in stereotyping or electrotyping. W. W. Pasko, *American Dictionary of Printing and Bookmaking*. New York: Howard Lockwood & Co., 1894.

The shallow mold in which the face of a type is cast; also the papier-mâché mold made from a page of type for stereotyping; the brass dies used on a typecasting machine. Hugo Hahn, *The Dictionary of Graphic Arts Terms*. Chicago: United Typothetae of America, 1928.

(1) In a typesetting machine, a brass plate having on its front edge an intaglio of a character it is to mold or produce in relief. (2) In type founding, a metal plate used as a mold to form the face of a type (3) In stereotyping and electrotyping, a plaster, wax, lead or papier-mâché mold containing an impression of a type form from which a plate is to be made. *Dictionary of Printing Terms*. Salt Lake City: Porte Publishing Co., 1950.

PATRIX =

The punch used in making letters, so called in contrast with the matrix, or matrices. *American Dictionary of Printing and Bookmaking*, 1894, op. cit.

In type founding, the pattern or die used to form the matrix which, in turn, forms the face of a type. *Dictionary of Printing Terms*, 1950, op. cit.

I

THE PRE-HISTORY OF MATRIX COMPOSING MACHINES

"Design, punch, matrix, type. These steps constituted the essentials of letter founding when the invention of movable types became an established reality almost five hundred years ago." These words are borrowed from R. Hunter Middleton's *Making Printers' Typefaces*, a small book privately printed and published in 1938 by the Black Cat Press in Chicago. It is one of the few books bearing on the subject of matrices and, while not a history, it does make a significant contribution to the knowledge of how matrices and metal types were made.

Going back to the beginning of the twentieth century, it is evident that historians of printing have neglected a fundamentally important subject relating to printing processes. This is the *composition matrix*, from which, beginning in the late 1880s, the printer has machine-composed and cast his body types instead of setting them by hand. Ironically, for all its success, the technology of this method has now almost disappeared, having enjoyed only a century's lifespan.

The *history* of printers' composing machines itself was not neglected in the early years of this century; several able authors, American and European, have endowed us with diverse writings on this subject. But with the exception of Legros and Grant's *Typographical Printing-Surfaces* (1916), these authors have overlooked writing about the very thing that made hot-metal composing machines possible—the matrix. One of the important books on printers' composing machines is John S. Thompson's *History of Composing Machines*, published in 1904, with excellent pictures of nearly every machine he mentioned and described. Nowhere in this book, however, are there any illustrations or discussions of matrices. Thompson merely mentions that a number of these machines used matrices.

As thorough and wide-ranging as typographic history has been, most writers apparently did not see the essential part that matrices played in the development of matrix-composing machines, or simply accepted the matrices as part of the inventions and did not consider them of historical importance. There is a probability (no fault of the historians) that the early inventors or manufacturers of these machines did not consider it "safe" to reveal technical details or manufacturing procedures—jealously protected by registered patents—because of rivalry, competition and the possibility of "piracy."

It is well known that the crucial development in the middle of the fifteenth century of the matrix for hand casting *movable types* (hereafter called single-types) is attributed to Johann Gutenberg, who thereby brought into being a more rapid and accurate means of increasing and disseminating knowledge through the medium of these movable types. In ancient times, hand-writing and inscribing were the only known methods by which relatively permanent records of important events and information could be made, but simultaneously another means was devised for preparing and perpetuating brief or significant pieces of information. This was by taking *repeatable impressions* from carved or engraved (relief or intaglio) stamping devices on clay tablets. Babylonian and Assyrian scribes and officials used this procedure for establishing ownership, recording business transactions, verifying royal or legal documents and personal matters. Later, these *seals* were used to mark papyrus and parchment documents, as well as other materials through the succeeding centuries. From those early times the relief *impressable image* in particular became well known and used in many ways, and was a direct forerunner of the relief printing-surfaces letterpress printers have been familiar with since Gutenberg's time. But there was a long time-lag between the invention of the seal and the mid-fifteenth century invention of *matrices* for casting single-types, one of the greatest technical achievements in man's history. Not until the mid-nineteenth century did the next great advancement occur with the invention of numerous machines which set (or were intended to set) the single-types previously hand-cast from type founders' matrices. The inevitable outcome of this new technology was the invention of other more complex machines which used *matrices* to make and compose types or type lines from hot metal (and on cold metal, too) for make-up into pages for printing books and newspapers.

Beginning about 1840, a large number of typesetting machines were subsequently developed which composed single-types (founders' types) and were specifically intended to replace or supplement the motions of the hand compositor. The enthusiastic inventors of those machines deserve a nostalgic handshake for their pioneering efforts, which, though sometimes eccentric and sometimes temporarily useful, were more often doomed to failure for reasons beyond their control. There was a long line of such inventors and generally the only surviving records of their experiments are found in complicated, hard-to-decipher patent specifications. Only about a dozen examples of early composing machines have survived in scaled-down patent models which are in the collections of the Smithsonian Institution, e.g., Mitchel, 1854; Loughborough, 1855; Felt, 1860; Fraser, 1862; Baer, 1866, Alden, 1868; De La Peña, 1870; Westcott, 1871; Pattyson, 1875; Burr, 1875; Dickinson, 1876.

Except for the complex, sometimes fuzzy specifications in the patents, only a handful of American inventors published full descriptions of their machines. Very little other documentation remains. And, of course, such books which were published are now very rare and expensive. There are two examples of this nature in my library: Oren L. Brown's *A Description of Brown's Patent Type Setting and Distributing Machinery* (Boston, 1870) is a slim volume of 42 pages and 5½ x 8¼ inches in size, which gives descriptions but no illustrations of the two machines, a type-setter and a distributor. Good illustrations can be seen in Ringwalt's *American Encyclopaedia of Printing*, pages 480, 481, Philadelphia, 1871. The other book is Charles C. Yeaton's colossal *Manual of the Alden Type-Setting and Distributing Machine*, 11¾ x 17½ inches, 246 pages, with 1159 illustrations (New York, 1865). This 8½-pound book has been noted for its colossal production cost of $11,000 to set up on the Alden machine and print and bind a mere 100 copies for stockholders, yet its large dimensions and many typographical intricacies are visible evidence of just why it cost so much money.

Printing from type had its European origin around 1440–1450, but like the more-or-less common style of wooden printing press that prevailed until the beginning of the nineteenth century, typesetting and hand composition remained virtually unchanged until the last two decades of that century. As brilliant as Gutenberg's achievements at Mainz, Germany, were, no later original advances were made in that country toward mechanical typesetting through the medium of matrices—Americans produced the first hot metal composing machines.

The early inventors of single-type machines showed that mechanical typesetting was really possible and better and faster machines emerged as the impracticable routes were eliminated or improved. Invariably, the early inventors made the innocent mistake of working with foundry-cast types; they were familiar only with the hand tradition and knew of no short cuts. It finally dawned on a few of them that types should be produced in the form of *totally manufactured composition in one machine*, without having to obtain types from established foundries. Thus, after a long period of experimentation and the expenditure of untold sums of money in abortive speculations and futile trials, the *composable matrix* was finally conceived in America in the mid–1880s, making it possible for each composing room to be literally its own type foundry. (Printing types consist of an alloy of lead, tin and antimony.)

Hand-made Punches

At this point something should be said about *how* the early matrices were made. Originally, *punches* for making single-types were hand-made by artists who served long apprenticeships. The punch (Fig. 1) carried the letter design which was first scratched *in reverse* on the flat end of a soft steel blank, which varied in thickness according to the size of the type desired, and was of a convenient length according to the will of the engraver. Then he engraved or carved the shape of the letter in the steel with small gravers (burins) of various sizes. Small watchmaker's or jeweler's files also were used to dress the outer edges. In certain cases a *counter-punch* was

used. This was a separately engraved steel punch representing the inner parts of certain letters, such as the inside of the B or the O. Driving this hardened counter-punch into the softer original steel blank eliminated the necessity of hand-carving or gouging out these inner parts, called "counters." After much tedious handwork in forming the shape of the character, checking the progress of the cutting by taking smoke proofs, by holding the engraved end of the punch over the

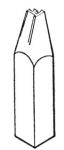

Fig. 1 Hand-cut punch. See Reference 7, p. 195.

flame of a candle or oil lamp, which left a carbon deposit, then "printing" on a piece of paper, tempering or hardening the engraved end, and finishing it to its final state, the punch was driven into the side of a bar of polished copper with a hammer. This then became the *strike*, or *drive*, which needed further refinement, called *justifying the matrix* before it could be used in a hand mold. The bulge caused by the strike had to be filed away; then it was lapped or rubbed smooth on a fine file or stone, followed by checking for depth of drive, levelness, squareness and letter alignment. Delicate hand instruments were used in these operations until the matrix was ready to fit into the mold. Even now further adjustments were sometimes necessary for hand-casting perfect types. When the matrix was ready for production, a slow process followed in which types were hand cast one at a time. By these time-honored means, punch cutters, matrix fitters, mold makers and type founders practiced their arts until the late nineteenth century. Sadly, the foregoing terms have now passed from the vocabulary of modern commercial printers.

During the years 1897–1900 a series of articles by William E. Loy on American "Designers and Engravers of Types" was published in *The Inland Printer* (Vols. 20–25). All told, twenty-eight essays were written on these type designers and hundreds of their type faces are named, as well as the foundries they worked for as employees, or as freelance artists. Except for this important run of articles, many designers and punch cutters of that era remained anonymous, even to printers. Notwithstanding the fact that tremendous skill and artistry were involved in their work, few if any were ever recognized or publicly named by the more than thirty competing American foundries at the time.

In 1896, the great Philadelphia type foundry of MacKellar, Smiths and Jordan issued its centennial keepsake book—a large, grand and elegant publication, beautifully printed in the foundry's specimen room. For all its pretentions and descriptions of the foundry and the art of type founding, there is never once any mention of a type designer or punch cutter's name. The closest the volume comes to this is found on page 64, ". . . to cut the punch or steel letter, for instance, not only requires an operator who is an engraver, and has a knowledge of the proportions and relations one printed letter should bear to another, but the steel has to be of the finest quality . . . and fitting the matrices is as fascinating as anything in the foundry, and to see a man cutting a punch and driving it into other metal, and examining and

correcting the impression, it looks as if everything depended upon the success of this operation."[1]

In his book, *Type Foundries of America and their Catalogs*, Maurice Annenberg says, "It is impossible to give an accurate biography of the early engravers, or punch cutters as they were called, because very meager records of their lives exist. Nor are records available of the type styles or faces they designed. The numerous fires in type foundries have destroyed all old records, and there are no documents or drawings. The early type founders purchased their original punches or matrices from Europe and for a long time there was no necessity for a punch cutter. The constant wear or accidents finally proved the value of making matrices in the United States, and Edwin Starr is recognized as the first to regularly engage in that occupation."[2] With the proliferation of American type foundries in the first half of the nineteenth century and the enormous demand for types, it soon became evident that there was an increasing domestic need for skilled punch cutters and matrix makers.

During the 1890s—and later—a popular type face originated by one foundry often ran the risk of becoming redundant, in that

1. *One Hundred Years, 1796–1896, MacKellar, Smiths and Jordan Foundry, Philadelphia, Pa.,* 1896. "To our Friends and Patrons this Souvenir is Respectfully Dedicated." The title page is made up of decorative foundry elements, printed in red, green, gold, and black. The page size is 11½ x 14½ inches and the binding is in white cloth over boards, stamped in gold, and brown ink. Article XXIII of W. E. Loy's series in *The Inland Printer,* Vol. 24 (Dec. 1899), p. 417, reveals that Charles Henry Beeler, Jr., cut the 7 point and 15 point sizes of *Ronaldson* for this book, a popular typeface at that time. This Souvenir Book has many finely printed scenes of the Foundry, and illustrations of a hand-cut punch and various molds, but Benton's pantographic engraving machine is not mentioned or displayed; evidently this famous Foundry in 1896 had not yet adopted the Benton machine.
2. Mr. Annenberg adapted this statement from Article XXV in W. E. Loy's series on the punch cutters of the early nineteenth century. See Reference 1.

it was copied by other foundries. A punch cutter could imitate a best-selling original design without license or permission, a practice which did not add distinction to the punchcutting profession. Another common practice was the plagiarism of a design by electrodepositing matrices from an original font of type; by the slight alteration on certain capitals with some hand tooling, a "new" design was "created." It was not unusual for three or four foundries to offer what appeared to be the same face, but with a different name or number from each foundry. However, with the revolutionary advent of keyboard matrix-composing machines and the use of mechanical engraving for meeting the punchcutting needs of those machines, the hand punchcutting profession became nearly obsolete.

The pitfalls of designing or bringing out new matrix faces were not ignored by the manufacturers of early matrix-composers. With revolutionary foresight and a good bit of empiricism they were reaching out into new typographic directions. Following the lead of Mergenthaler, they created the "Printing Revolution," an achievement which changed the face of American newspaperdom more than any other social or industrial upheaval in the nineteenth century.

Due to the genetive nature of this development—in the absence of documented evidence—one can assume that at first it was not critically important for the manufacturers to seek out and hire designers of type faces for the new composing machines, because the founders had already led the way with scores of practical type faces. Here was an easy "out" for the manufacturers of composition matrices; since there was such an abundance of popular designs to choose from, with which both printers and the public were familiar, making "new" designs was

unnecessary. It was, therefore, only natural to turn to this source. Perhaps this is why the following comment is made by Richard N. McArthur in *The Book of OZ Cooper*: "In truth the oldtime type founders had been guilty of taking from each other, and *the typesetting machine makers all got their starts by taking over bodily the best-selling foundry faces*.[3] (my italics). This statement does not really tell much in respect to "the typesetting machine makers," but, if they did take "over bodily the best-selling foundry faces," they had to have a means of reproducing them in composable matrix form. They seem to have been reticent on this point.

Prior to the use of the Benton matrix-engraving machine, the Mergenthaler Printing Company in Brooklyn had difficulties in making good matrices from hand-cut punches. In the "Report of the Board of Directors" of January 21, 1888, it is stated "The matrix problem has been solved. The matrices are by no means perfect yet, but the defects are largely due to defective dies; and by a contract recently completed with Benton, Waldo & Co., of Milwaukee, for the mechanical cutting of these dies, it is believed that absolute accuracy in the *reproduction of the best styles of types* (my italics) can now be secured. The alignment is greatly improved." Richard McArthur's remark in *The Book of OZ Cooper* is thus proved true.

However, at this late date (1985) it is but conjectural that the early composing machine makers were willing to give credit to any particular "type designers," as such. Perhaps this was because good designs were

3. From an essay by Richard N. McArthur in *The Book of OZ Cooper, An Appreciation of Oswald Bruce Cooper*. Chicago: The Society of Typographic Arts, 1949, p. 71. Oswald Bruce Cooper, 1879–1940, was one of the best graphic artists in that era; he designed several type faces of note and popularity. See Reference 10.

already available from the type founders and that the name of a designer or punch cutter was not considered essential to the sale of matrices. The composing machines themselves could not be operated without the matrices, so here was the impulse which pushed for matrices regardless of their point of origin. Only years later when such artists as William A. Dwiggins, Frederic W. Goudy, Rudolph Ruzicka, Sol Hess, and others, became famous as type designers for matrix-composing machines, did the manufacturers connect their names to the sale of composition matrices. During the 1930s and 1940s, designs commissioned by the dominant manufacturers and advertised as the work of these artists sold more matrices than ever before.

This is not to say that in these later years the manufacturers of matrix-using machines did not acquaint the printers with their methods of making matrices, for it was considered important that printers should know as much about the matrices as they did about the machines that used them. The manufacturers' finely printed promotional and advertising literature contained many illustrations and descriptions of the procedures followed in the factories' laboratories and matrix-making departments.

With the actual, or proposed, introduction of matrix-using machines in the late 1880s, successful or not, a direct result of the transition of machine-set types to machine-set matrices was the creation of a new problem: this was the manufacture of large quantities of matrices for composing machines instead of types. The difficulties that Mergenthaler faced were typical of those faced by other inventors, all of whom had to find ways to produce their matrices economically. At this point in their development, making matrices by a non-mechanical method was extremely expensive, and the inventors of matrix-using machines were forced to contend with these difficulties as long as they had to depend on hand-cut punches.

The following two paragraphs are paraphrased from *Biography of Ottmar Mergenthaler*[4] by Carl Otto Schoenrich:

The most difficult problem connected with manufacturing the matrices at first was their production at a price not prohibitive. To give an example of the discouragement he met with in these attempts, the following incident may be mentioned: Mr. Mergenthaler, in an attempt to enlist outside help, called upon Mr. J. Ryan, a well known type founder in Baltimore. He showed Mr. Ryan some of the matrices he had made and told him that the machine required about twelve hundred of them and that they had to be produced at a cost of 6¢ or less. Mr. Ryan took one of his own foundry matrices and commenced to laugh, and said, "Young man, you see this matrix? It is one of our standard matrices, and as you see, it is a much simpler piece of work than yours. Now, we pay from fifty cents to a dollar apiece [just] for the work of adjusting it after the impression has been made. If you can produce these matrices for the typefounders at fifty cents apiece, there is a fortune in store for you on that line alone and you need not waste your energy in useless attempts to make impossibilities. Assuming that your machine as such is a success, yet it is

4. *Biography of Ottmar Mergenthaler and the History of the Linotype, Its Invention and Development*. Baltimore: The Friedenwald Company, 1898, pp. 27, 28. See Reference 19.

bound to fail on the cost of the matrices if for no other reason."

This discouragement and similar answers from other sources left no other option for Mergenthaler but to go ahead and solve the problem himself. He devoted several months of concentrated effort to this part of the business, for which some thirty special machines and machine attachments were required and installed in a special plant for this purpose. This was the production of his matrices on a commercially feasible scale; it was a great achievement and became the pride of Mr. Mergenthaler.[5] One great difficulty in his matrix department was the expense and trouble of maintaining the original steel stamps which produced the matrices proper. No machine existed at that time which could engrave these stamps at small cost with the certainty of maintaining the same size and shape, since they were engraved by hand at a cost of $5 per piece, and their accuracy was far inferior to those later produced by the Benton engraving machine.

In 1886, the first year in which the *Linotype* was operating in the composing room of the New York *Tribune*, Mergenthaler had written a letter to the editor Whitelaw Reid, explaining his progress on additional machines that the "Mergenthaler Printing Company," a syndicate of newspaper publishers, had ordered from his Baltimore factory. One of his comments in this letter, dated Baltimore, September 11, 1886, is quoted thus: "The steel Type [punches] for the Nonpareil [6-point] are done and Mr. West is just now starting on the Agate [5½-point]. He can not get them done within a month, but I am satisfied he will get them done by

the time we can make use of them. . . . If we can get another Type cutter of somewhat less pretensions than Mr. West it would probably be well to have him" [the other Type cutter].[6] There was a James West who had come from Scotland and worked as a punch cutter for several different type founders in New York. A brief outline of his career may be found in W. E. Loy's "Designers and Engravers of Type," No. II, *The Inland Printer*, Vol. 20, (March 1898). He could well have been Mergenthaler's punch cutter.

Without the help of the Benton pantograph, it was impossible to achieve the quality and accuracy—and economy—that Mergenthaler was endeavoring to produce. At this period in the history of the *Linotype* (1887),[7] Mergenthaler was working under great difficulties with the Syndicate who had established a separate factory in Brooklyn and were trying to build and monopolize the "Blower" Linotype (crude as it was) in their composing rooms. A great deal of bitterness and unfair treatment had been heaped on Mergenthaler, mainly because he wanted to improve

5. Evidently this was before Linn B. Benton's pantographic engraving machine became available, but Mergenthaler's methods are not revealed in this account.
6. I am indebted to Corban Goble, Ph.D., Berea, Kentucky, for this information, which is among the papers of Whitelaw Reid in the Library of Congress, #148390–92. Mergenthaler's estimated cost of 6¢ per matrix was probably very reasonable. After fifty-seven years of improvement in matrices and their manufacturing methods—1934—the Company was selling 2-letter matrices at 10¢ each, not a large advancement in price after all those years. This information comes from the Company's *Useful Matrix Information and Price List* booklet 610.11–8–34.
7. It was in this year of the "infancy" of the *Linotype* that the New York *Tribune* published the *first book* set on the "Blower"—*The Tribune Book of Open-Air Sports*. This is a 500-page book and considering the problems with the machine and its sometimes erratic matrix actions, it is a good demonstration of what this first matrix-composing machine could do in the field of book printing.

the machine—which they objected to—and he eventually resigned from the Company, of which he was a small stockholder. Mergenthaler believed the machine could be greatly improved and, working on a new design in his Baltimore factory, the first "Square-Base" model was produced in 1889. This model was radically different in appearance from the "Blower" and was a far better and faster machine. It was followed by the "Simplex" Linotype in 1890, also called "Model 1," and the ultimate for which Mergenthaler had been striving for over ten years. It remained the foundation model for subsequent Linotype development and many Model 1 machines continued in use for the next thirty years. Fuller descriptions and illustrations of these machines are in my book, *The Development of Printers' Mechanical Typesetting Methods, 1822–1925.*

A vitally important part of Mergenthaler's work at that time was also spent in improving his methods of making matrices, although he still had to depend on the hand-cut punches. He had already *designed* an engraving maachine, but no details of it are given in the *Biography*. When the Benton machine became known Mergenthaler abandoned his efforts in this direction.[8]

The greatest shortcoming of the hand punch was its fragility and delicacy of cutting, and could easily be marred by repeated or careless manual use; if it did become damaged it was virtually impossible to re-cut it exactly. The hand punch was cut by eye using manual tools, not engraved by tracing from a master pattern, set and rigid in its contours. Mass production of matrices on a commercial scale was a greater obstacle for Mergenthaler (and other inventors) to overcome than building a line-casting machine. However, the problem was suddenly solved with

the use of a device originally invented with an entirely different purpose in mind.

Machine-cut Punches

A most fortunate circumstance took place in the year 1885—the same year that Mergenthaler announced his "Blower" Linotype—when the Milwaukee type founder Linn Boyd Benton patented a *pantographic matrix-engraving machine* (see illustration). It was soon discovered that with a slight altera-

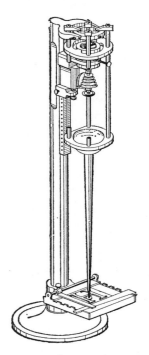

Fig. 2 Benton matrix/punch cutting machine, from patent drawing. See Reference 7, p. 196.

8. These details are related in *Biography of Ottmar Mergenthaler*, especially on pages 26–28. In answer to an inquiry to Mike Parker (formerly of the Mergenthaler Linotype Company) on their early methods of matrix production, the following note was received: "I do not believe any such records survive. Tradition at the Mergenthaler Linotype Company holds that (1) Matrices used for development of the first machines were stamped from hand cut punches. (2) When volume production was attempted, replacement of broken punches with identical copies became a major problem which (3) availability of the Benton pantographic punch cutter solved. I do not have more." Thus this source which should have been rich in archival material seems to have dried up.

tion this machine could cut punches equally as well as matrices, but several years were to elapse before Mergenthaler could use it. The machine was patented in the United States under #327,855, and in England under #11,894. However, there are at least three notices in trade journals stating the prior use of "engraving machines" for cutting punches for foundry matrices. The oldest evidence of such a machine was reported by Robert Wiebking, a well known Chicago engraver and punch cutter who prior to 1909 had told Nicholas J. Werner of the Inland Type Foundry in St. Louis that his father in Germany had used a matrix-engraving machine in 1875 and possibly as early as 1870,[9] but nothing since is known of it. If Benton's invention could have been said to be derivative, it must be considered so with the probability that Benton was not aware of the Wiebking machine and, therefore, can be considered an American invention of a high order, justly deserving the credit it has been given in typographic history. Nor did it remain a static invention, for all the principal type founders and composing machine makers adopted it eventually and improved it in various ways.

Linn Boyd Benton originally used "sorts" *patterns* for cutting soft-metal "dummy" matrices from which electrotype matrices were made, in order to replace worn or damaged matrices in his foundry, thereby avoiding the necessity for hand-cutting the punches.[10] The machine was designed with this purpose in mind and it is quite possible that Benton did not anticipate the enormous and widespread use his invention was later put to in the type casting industry. It was, in fact, an important breakthrough for the type founders, as well as for the newly developing matrix-composing machine makers, and

the full industrial impacts on each will be shown hereafter. The earlier reports on the use of engraving machines notwithstanding, it has been said that cutting punches had not occurred to Benton until a Mergenthaler Company representative suggested such a possibility.[11] This was a stroke of good for-

9. The fact that Benton patented his engraving machine in 1885 is not an indication that he had invented it in that year. There was often a lapse of two to five years between application for a patent and the date of its issue, and this may have been the case with the Benton machine. Other than Robert Wiebking's statement there are two prior notices of "engraving machines" in trade journals: in 1932 Nicholas J. Werner of the former Inland Type Foundry told Edmund G. Gress, editor of *The American Printer*, that William Schraudstadter at the old Central Type Foundry in St. Louis had "operated a punch-cutting machine as early as 1882 in his father's foundry. . . . Being one of the first to carry out direct engraving with such a machine, which lacked precision and required to be supplemented by hand work." This information is in "The Inland Type Foundry, 1894–1911," by Dr. James Eckman, *Printing & Graphic Arts*, Vol. VIII, 1960, p. 31; Lunenburg, Vermont: The Stinehour Press. It is not stated who built this engraving machine. The other prior notice (concerning Benton's machine) is in *Paper and Printing Trades Journal*, September 1884, No. 48, p. 10; London: Field & Tuer: "Benton, Waldo & Co. Milwaukee, claim to have perfected a machine for cutting punches for original characters for type foundries in steel— . . . It will cut from the largest to the smallest punch—even to half-diamond; . . . a piece of work now requiring four hours to perfect by the hand process can, under its operation, be turned out in half an hour." This could imply that Benton's machine originated in 1883, or in 1884.

10. Dr. James Eckman, *The Heritage of the Printer*. Philadelphia: North American Publishing Co., 1965, p. 111.

11. This representative is said to have been Philip T. Dodge, a Company official. As a result, the Mergenthaler Printing Company (a rather odd name for a manufacturer of composing machines) in Brooklyn promptly made arrangements with Benton for the use of his engraving machine. Since Mergenthaler's separate plant in Baltimore was the laboratory where his own version of matrices was being developed, the Brooklyn plant, under the direction of Editor Whitelaw Reid, preceded Mergenthaler in the use of the Benton machine. Corban Goble, Berea, Kentucky, who has done extensive research on "The Obituary of A Machine: The Rise and Fall of Ottmar Mergenthaler's Linotype At U. S. Newspapers," has told me in a personal letter that "The first Benton Machine was shipped to the Brooklyn factory early in 1889." Just when Mergenthaler was able to acquire a Benton machine for the Baltimore plant has so far remained elusive.

tune for hot metal type casting, and typography in general.

For the first time, a pre-designed letterform, prepared by an artist, in enlarged size *in relievo* for use in the engraving machine was required. No matter how many times it was used, this master pattern remained unchanged and thus countless punches, exact duplicates of each other, could be made. "In cutting the punch, the tracer [of the pantograph] follows around the pattern character, leaving the punch character in relief in reversed position."[12] Additionally, the engraving machine is adjustable for different sizes, within certain limitations, without changing the proportions, and the rapidly revolving cutting tool at the top of the machine interprets the motions of the tracer accurately. The Benton pantograph, therefore, enabled varying sizes of the same design to be duplicated with a degree of precision and speed not possible with the time consuming manual processes of former days.

Although invented by a type founder, the pantograph engraver ultimately was far more useful, indeed, essential, to devices employing the composition matrix than to the traditional type founder.[13] A short review of the role of the punch and the matrix in each process will be helpful to understand this statement:

In the type foundry, the hand punch was used to *drive* a matrix. Although it could be damaged in the process, most often it was not. Rather than the punch, the matrix bore the pounding of constant use day after day in the type casting molds. Occasionally foundry matrices would burn out or otherwise be rendered useless; in these instances new matrices were driven from the original punches. Only infrequently were new punches required and that is why the old type

foundry was able to tolerate the slow, laborious processes required to manufacture the hand punch.

On the other hand, with the developing composition-matrix machines, many duplicates of matrices were required for each machine, multiplied by the number of machines sold. Consequently, a broken punch was a great problem—an intolerable one—because of the great time required to re-cut the punch using hand methods. Benton's machine minimized this problem by making it possible to mechanically duplicate a damaged punch in a short time. And thus the great pressure of production of matrices for composing machines was moved to the punch. This was the situation in 1889.

Benton's engraving machine was the kind of labor-saving tool sorely needed by the type-making industry, yet its invention was the eventual undoing of the type founding industry so far as hand-set body types were concerned, since the production of large numbers of mechanical matrix-composition machines was now both possible and practical. The new and soon-to-be-available matrix machines were poised to steal away the "life blood" of the foundries, that is, their enormous and lucrative trade in composition body types, which up to this point all newspaper and book printers in the nation were obliged to set by hand in their composing rooms.[14] The trade of the hand compositor

12. R. Hunter Middleton, *Making Printers' Typefaces.* Chicago: The Black Cat Press, 1938, p. 25. The proprietor of The Black Cat Press was Norman Forgue.

13. The type founder was relieved of the tedious chore of cutting punches by hand, for now he could engrave his matrices directly; on the other hand the matrix-maker could now machine engrave his punches, the hand-made product no longer being necessary.

14. In this period a number of hand-operated or power-driven single-type setting machines were in use,

was on the brink of obsolescence, for his livelihood was about to be eliminated or turned into a machine function, a situation created by the advent of the composition matrix. It made the compositor into a machine operator, taught him new skills, increased his work output, and, fortunately, enlarged his ranks.

Ten years later, Mergenthaler's company in Baltimore was known as OTT. MERGENTHALER AND CO., Mechanical Engineers and Machinists. Their *Catalogue A*, issued in 1898, is quite descriptive of the factory (where the original Model 1 had been built), and its specialties, including the manufacture of spare Linotype parts. Though the Syndicate in Brooklyn years earlier had refused to accept Mergenthaler's experiments with *"steel" matrices*, he had not given up, and the following announcement appears on page 153 of Catalogue A: . . . "we have been engaged for a number of years in efforts to produce matrices of better wearing qualities than those made of brass. . . . We now have solved the problem by using soft steel and hardening the matrix around the impression point, as indicated in the cut at *a*, which is the most delicate portion of the matrix and containing the fine side walls that encircle the letter." This small steel element was inset into the brass body of the matrix carrier, as in the cut (see illustration). Presumably, by this time Mergenthaler was using the Benton engraving machine to cut his punches.

The economic and technical benefits of the Benton engraving machine are best exempli-

fied in the massive *Specimen Book of Type Styles*, published by the Mergenthaler Linotype Company in 1915. The Foreword in this book of 1078 pages states "At our Factory and at our Agencies throughout the world are carried a stock of over one hundred million finished matrices for prompt service of the owners of the 33,000 Linotypes in use." Furthermore, the importance of Benton's machine for this manufacturer is shown by the fact that over twelve hundred faces and special characters are listed and illustrated in this book. But the Mergenthaler specimen book is only one such example, for the competing matrix-composing machine manufacturers were also publishing their catalogs and specimen sheets, equally indebted to Benton's genius. The Benton machine, which by this time had been improved

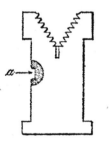

Fig. 2a Mergenthaler "steel" matrix. See Reference 13, p. 153.

and had changed its appearance, proved to be of great value for the type founders in other ways, especially for their trade in display (large) types, and in a myriad of designs and sizes of pictorial "type cuts" which printers found useful in so many ways.

By 1915 the *Linotype* and the *Monotype* were the two dominant matrix-using machines. The *Linotype* now had competition in the *Linograph* and the *Intertype*, but the *Monotype* had no competition at all, the

---

especially in the newspaper industry, and included the Simplex One-Man Typesetter; and the Kastenbein; Hattersley; Dow; Cox; Empire; Chadwick; and Fraser typesetters.

only other single-type casting machine, the Goodson *Graphotype*, having faded away.

Benton's pantographic engraver was the means by which the type-casting industry was liberated from the archaic days of hand-cutting punches, making it possible to mass produce the matrices for these amazing matrix-composers. However, the art of the hand punch cutter must not be belittled or regarded as superseded, for his work was considered (and still is by discerning typophiles) the acme of fine type-making, the epitome of form and proportion, qualities not always found in mechanically cut punches for machine composition. By the third and fourth decades of this century, the high point had been reached by designers and manufacturers of type faces for slug or single-type cast-ing. Many of their designs are still popular, and in numerous instances have been converted for use in phototypesetting equipment. Even during that period of its greatest triumphs, the theory had been proposed that mechanical punchcutting could not interpret the spirit of the artist's conception with the same fidelity possible in hand engraving, that the movement and sparkle of the hand technique was submerged in mechanical symmetry. Though this theory was justified to some extent, it was not through the fault of the engraving machine, but rather to a lack of its intelligent and sympathetic use.[15]

15. The statements in the last part of this paragraph are derived from *The Linotype Development of Type Faces*, by C. H. Griffith. Brooklyn: Mergenthaler Linotype Company, 1938.

II

A NEW APPROACH TO MACHINE TYPESETTING

In the latter part of the nineteenth century a number of inventors realized that setting previously cast single-types by machinery was the wrong approach. They began to experiment with machines that first composed matrices and then cast the types with "hot" metal, an entirely new concept. The resulting transitions from machines setting single-types to machines setting or moving matrices were quite varied and amazing. Although many forms of matrix-using machines were invented and patented, only a few of them were able finally to reach the marketplace, and fewer still were those which were successful enough to endure continual use in printers' composing rooms.

With the exception of a British patent by Joseph Mazzini for a "Uniplane" system in 1843,[1] Charles Westcott's machine invented in 1871 (U. S. Patent #115,797) is the first recorded American attempt to compose matrices. (According to Antoine Seyl, in his Belgian history of typographic composing machines, Westcott's machine had been exhibited at the Centennial Exposition at Philadelphia in 1876. See Reference 19.1.) Between 1871 and 1915 there was a great deal of overlap between single-type and matrix-setting systems. Some resembled each other, while others differed radically. The handwriting was on the wall, and the few single-type setters that did meet with some success —the last being the *Unitype* of 1902—were faced with constantly improving matrix-setters that promised to make them all obsolete.

It is à propos to say that many of those early machines were wildly impractical, even mind-boggling, which contributed to their failure, while others, based on sounder mechanical principles, proved more effective and economical than hand-setting—such were the early machines of Mergenthaler, Lanston, Goodson, Scudder, Rogers, and Pedersen.[2] These men all saw great possibilities in their machines, though each worked along different mechanical lines. In improved forms all of these machines successfully competed in the marketplace for some years, but only a handful, namely, some models of the *Linotype* (and the *Intertype*) and Lanston's *Monotype* have survived the test of time. The *Intertype* (plate VII) is a derivative of the *Linotype* and is here considered in that class.

Peculiar ideas often proved fatal to the development of some of the early machines, but the manufacture of their matrices, on the other hand, was undoubtedly a major stumbling block. An inventor's misguided enthusiasm or his lack of insight into both manufacturing problems and printers' composition problems often doomed his device. There were many more non-printer inventors of those machines than there were printer-inventors. As engineers or inspired machine designers they were trying to help in a direction that printers sometimes did not believe

1. Joseph Mazzini (nationality uncertain), British patent #9731, issued in the year 1843, "being partly a communication from a Foreigner residing abroad."
2. Ottmar Mergenthaler, *Linotype*; Tolbert Lanston, *Monotype*; George Goodson, *Graphotype*; John R. Rogers, *Typograph*; Hans Pedersen, *Linograph*. See Richard E Huss, *The Development of Printers' Mechanical Typesetting Methods, 1822–1925*. Charlottesville, Virginia: The University Press of Virginia, 1973.

in or mistrusted; yet many progressive printers encouraged these inventors. Many impressive ideas were proposed, though there was, occasionally, a lack of typographical understanding, not to mention financial backing for the "amateurs." Too often, the development of matrix-using machines was challenging, costly, difficult, and, ultimately, disappointing. For a hundred years, from 1822 (the date of William Church's machines[3]) scientific and mechanical principles were persistently investigated from many angles. Yet, for most of these enthusiasts success was frustratingly elusive.

A lengthy discussion of the chronological development of various machines could serve no useful purpose here; the reader is, therefore, referred to two Appendices for a complete chronology. In consulting these Appendices it is important to note that every listing does not necessarily represent some completely new development. During the last two decades of the nineteenth century, inventors were sometimes in the employ of established manufacturers of these composing machines, not working independently. The so-called "inventions" frequently were merely improvements in existing machines rather than substantial breakthroughs, and often were absorbed into the experimental studies. Other patents were obtained by "loners," who as individuals did not have the financial means to bring their inventions to fruition, or sold their patents to dominant manufacturers, who often "shelved" them, when they could not be used as practical improvements.

Of the 59 patrix machines in Appendix A, 22 are known to have been built, but their commercial success, if any, at the time is now unknown. Matrix class machines were rather more successful; of the 107 machines listed in Appendix B, 54 passed the construction and experimental stages and became working devices. In time, this number was drastically reduced by advancing technology and frequent absorptions, so that about 1910 there were approximately ten matrix-composing machines available in America, with about the same number available in Europe. Some of these had originated in America, but most soon faded from the market.

By Way of Explanation to Lay Readers

Lay readers may wonder about the operations of some of the machines mentioned, but such details would extend this treatise beyond its limits. It would be appropriate to discuss, at least, representatives of the three *classes* of hot-metal systems that are or were used by many thousands of printers throughout the years of this century.

The *Linotype*, directly responsible for the "Printing Revolution" which occurred during the 1880s and 1890s, was re-designed and again improved by Mergenthaler in 1890. Its matrices were contained in an inclined magazine (Fig. 2.1) while the 90 keys on the keyboard controlled 90 different channels in the magazine, each channel containing a row of identical matrices. Fingering the keys operated escapement mechanisms which released the matrices one after another to drop onto an inclined traveling belt where they were carried in their proper order into an assembler to the left of the operator, double-wedge spacers (called space-bands) being inserted between the words. Upon completion of a line in the assembler, the operator pressed a lever to the right of the

3. Huss, *Dr. Church's "Hoax"*. Willow Street (sic), Penna. 17584: Graphic Crafts, Inc., 1976.

keyboard, which raised the line to the transfer channel, where it passed to the casting mechanism. Here the line was clamped in a "vise" which locked the matrices against the mold and then a shot of molten type-metal was forced into the mold against the matrices. The newly cast "slug" cooled instantly and was ejected from the mold onto the galley (tray) at the front of the machine. The line of matrices was then raised by an elevator to the top of the machine where the matrices

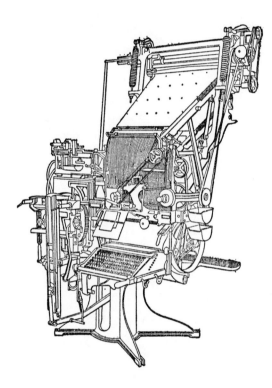

Fig. 2.1 Early Linotype machine, with recessed slug cast by later model.

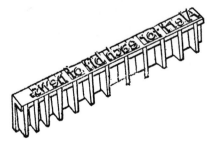

were re-distributed into the magazine by means of a series of combination teeth in the tops of the matrices and a ward-rail at the top of the magazine. In short, three operations took place in turn in the *Linotype*—composing, casting, and distributing—all moving along smoothly as the operator manipulated the keyboard. Thomas A. Edison called the *Linotype* the Eighth Wonder of the modern world.

Though quite different in construction, other makes of circulating-matrix machines followed these basic functions, some casting single-types, others slugs. Because of construction variations, these machines usually required different styles of matrices, which will be described later. After Mergenthaler's patents ran out in 1912, the *Linograph* (Plate V), and the *Intertype* (Plate VII), both became successful and efficient line casting machines. These two machines conformed to all the basic standards for line-slug work, but they were built on simplified principles and were less costly than the *Linotype*. Since 1915, the *Typocrat*, 1921, the *Supertype*, 1922, and the *Standard Compositor*, 1925, were offered briefly to the printing industry and were the last attempts made by Americans to introduce variant competitive matrix-composing machines. See Reference 5.

The *Monotype* system followed a principle entirely different from that of the *Linotype*. It had a certain affinity to hand-setting foundry types, since it cast single-types, which for other applications could be set by hand, and therein originated the name *Monotype*. The starting point was a specially designed separate keyboard with a key arrangement similar to the standard typewriter, but about four times larger. Different styles of Monotype keyboards contained from 150 to 250 keys, each keyboard used for a different class of composition. Coded combination holes were punched in a moving paper ribbon, representing each character and space. When text composition was completed, the ribbon was transferred to the casting machine (Fig. 2.2) where by means of compressed air, the Monotype die-case—a rectangular frame which held the matrices in rows—was shifted in two directions, so that each matrix cell (Fig. 17) would in turn be in correct position over the mold. The opening in the mold was automatically controlled by the message in the paper ribbon and a series of wedges regulated the "set-width" for each letter and the spaces, all of which, at the keyboard, were calculated on a "unit" system. As the types were cast, they were ejected from the mold and pushed through a delivery channel to the galley.

Although the *Ludlow* system is not included within the scope of this book, it is still an important composition method. Ludlow matrices are made of brass, driven from punches, as shown in Fig. 22, and are arranged in alphabetical order in cases similar to the regular foundry type *cap* case. The cases are inclined in the cabinets so the matrices will always stay in an upright position and arranged in tiers in each box. (Fig. 2.3) Using a special hollow composing stick, the operator slips the matrices from the boxes with his right thumb and index finger, gathering several matrices in each "lift" and drops them into the stick. Spacing is accomplished by inserting brass spaces between the words, ranging from ½-point to 12-point,[4] the larger spacers or "quads" being in multiples of a pica (the standard of measurement) up to 12 picas wide. The sticks are callibrated in picas and the lines are set to the desired measure. The Ludlow method has the additional advantage of setting long display lines in one

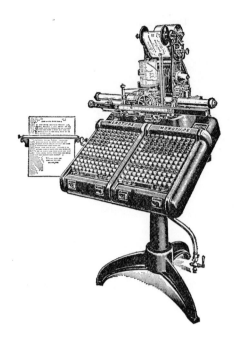

Fig. 2.2 Early Monotype keyboard and caster. Illustrations courtesy Richard L. Hopkins, Terre Alta, West Virginia.

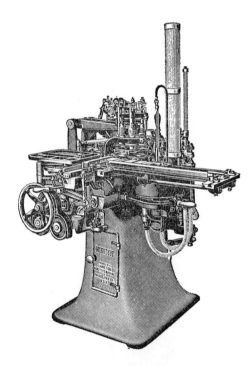

4. Point: printers' measurements are based on the *point* which is .01385″; 12 points equal 1 pica, 6 picas equal slightly less than 1″ (.9972″).

measure up to 112½ picas and subsequently casting the line in sections without showing breaks or gaps between the cast letters. The casting is done in a simple machine (Fig. 2.3), which can accommodate matrices up to 84-point sizes. After the slug is cast the operator re-distributes the matrices into the case and proceeds to set and cast the next line.

Fig. 2.3 Early Ludlow Typograph. See *American Printer*, Sesqui-Centennial number, July 1926, p. 29.

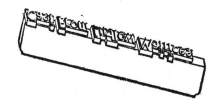

Slug cast by the Ludlow machine.

III

DEVELOPMENT OF
MATRIX-USING MACHINES

The expression "typesetting machines" is a common one to most printers. Matrix-using machines are not typesetters in the strictest mechanical sense, but are *matrix-setters* or *matrix-shifters*. Of all the many matrix-using *systems* conceived of or offered to printers eighty to ninety years ago, only three are still in universal use—the *circulating matrix*, from 1886; the *shiftable matrix*, from 1887; and the *handset matrix*, from 1911.[1]

Historically, the first proposed use of matrices for *mechanical typesetting* dates to 1822 with the original inventions of the American William Church, a medical doctor turned mechanical engineer.[2] Church's system contained three separate, but related, elements: a rapid typecaster, a typsetter, and a press, but we are concerned here only with the first two machines. All three were patented at the same time in England under #4664 in 1822. The typecaster was designed to use special individual matrices for the production of what would now be called "monotypes," and the keyboard-operated typesetter composed these types for printing newspapers or books. After printing, the types were to be thrown back into the melting-pot for re-casting in the typecaster, establishing the principle of "circulation," thereby eliminating hand distribution and anticipating all other non-distribution systems by about sixty-five years.

Thus Dr. Church established an original

mechanical typesetting concept: through the use of matrices he supplied disposable, inexpensive types. However, in the use of *single movable matrices* he was preceded by Louis-Robert Herhan (1768–1854), a printer in Paris, France, who invented the *first individually composable matrices* in 1798.[3] But Herhan's method could not be considered *mechanical*. He first made his matrices in the ends of copper bodies, which he drove from untempered hand-cut punches[4] in a small machine he built for this purpose. The "types" were recessed (intaglio[5]) instead of being in relief,[6] really being matrices, and were hand-set in the composing stick in reverse order because the "faces" were right-reading. High spaces were used between the matrices comprising the words to prevent metal running in and printing black spots from the cast plates. When the page forms were completed, type metal was poured over them producing stereotype plates; then the matrices were distributed into the case in the usual way and repeatedly hand-set to make more page-matrices.

Only Joseph Mazzini[7] in 1843 proposed a similar plan, but his method *was* mechanical. By first driving his punches into *type-metal blanks*, using a method similar to Herhan's, these matrices were then to be composed in a "Uniplane" matrix-setting machine until a

---

1. The handset matrix (Ludlow or Nebitype) is not dealt with in this book because it is handset in the same manner as individual types. This removes it from the general category of machine-composed matrices, but nevertheless it is still important as a matrix composition system.
2. Dr. William Church (1779–1863), native of Vermont, established operating principles in his machine that are still used today. See *Dr. Church's "Hoax,"* Reference 6.
3. See George A. Kubler, *Historical Treatises, Abstracts and Papers on Stereotyping.* New York: Geo. A. Kubler, 1936, p. 107.
4. See Fig. 1.
5. Below the flat surface of the casting element, as a cameo.
6. *Relief* means standing up, as in a rubber stamp.
7. See Huss, *Development*.

complete page had been composed. This type metal page-matrix was then locked up and put into a casting machine of Mazzini's design and a plate was cast. After casting the plates, the whole set of page-matrices could be "held for future re-use," or melted down, another version of the non-distribution principle.[8] A new supply of type-matrices then had to be made and composed into pages for the next job. It is not known if this system was ever put into use. It did, however, hint at the use of composable matrices for casting types.

These fore-runners of the machine-manipulated matrix followed two distinct lines of reasoning: a) Church was proposing precast types made from individual matrices in a separate type-casting machine in such a way as to cast whole alphabets or a plurality of types at each stroke of the plunger. This theory was later developed into a practical operation for a number of single-type setters using the non-distribution principle; b) Herhan and Mazzini both were more interested in the production of stereotype plates through the use of composable matrices. Their machines were not *directly* connected to the method by which composition was accomplished, and their theories were all but forgotten until revived later by some rather enthusiastic inventors of page-matrix methods who thought they had worked out practical answers to the printers' composition problems.

8. This means eliminating the labor of returning the types to the type case, a hand operation.

IV

PROBLEMS OF MATRIX MANUFACTURE

This chapter does not go into the finer details of the actual engineering and mechanical processes used in the production of composition matrices. My purpose here is to elaborate on the historic, economic, social, personal and outwardly descriptive aspects, more from a literary than an engineering point of view. One correspondent[1] asked if my "findings are more up-to-date." In a sense, they are just the opposite, since there is scarcely any possibility now of further improvements in matrix or foundry casting systems. "Up-to-date" can now only be applied to *type imaging* systems totally at variance with our topic here, while readers interested in the technical side of this subject should consult Legros and Grant's *Typographical Printing-Surfaces*, the best and most comprehensive study on the production of matrices.[2]

As diverse and ingenious as the many "typesetters" were, so were their matrices different from each other. Of the many that I have investigated, it seems that no two inventors designed or used the same style or form of matrix. Once the style or pattern of a matrix had been decided on, the manufacturing problem began.[3] To make matrices for a machine with commercial potential, matrix manufacturing procedures had first to be planned, designed and implemented. Stock materials, such as sheet or strip brass or copper, or bar stock, were readily available. Companies were established, vast capital

resources were obtained through the sale of stocks and bonds and factories were erected to produce the machines and their matrices. The pages of *The Inland Printer* before 1901 frequently contained stories of these companies and pictures of their factories.

It was necessary to design and build special machines, and tools, or adapt already existing ones, for making the matrices—lathes, millers, grinders, shavers, borers, *punch-presses*, indexing and measuring gauges and micrometric testing instruments.[4] The cornerstone of the matrix manufacturing process was Benton's matrix (or punch) engraving machine, which accelerated their production and greatly lowered their cost. Many lessons had to be learned, including the fact that extremely critical manufacturing tolerances had to be maintained in order to assure matrices that would produce types as accurate in every way as foundry types. This required dozens of inspections and tests before the matrices could be released on the market.

Personnel had to be trained and gain experience in order to do this work properly, for in the 1880s and 1890s this was an entirely new field opening up in the manufacturing area of the printing industry. In addition to these massive start-up costs, manufacturers had to develop sales and distribution methods and advertise widely. Many first-time inventors may not have been aware of these factors when they proposed their ideas for a machine or went to a machine shop with their plans. One of the probable reasons so few matrix-composing machines met with success was

1. Arvind M. Patel, a type founder, Ahmedabad, India.
2. Garland Publishing Company, 545 Madison Ave., New York, N.Y. 10012, has republished this book in hard cover.
3. See the chapter on "Matrices," in *Typographical Printing-Surfaces*, pp. 216–240, Reference 7.
4. Ibid., pp. 208, 213, 314; see also American patent listing 627,160 on p. 641.

that the manufacturer of the machine also had to be the manufacturer of the matrices, an inseparable combination. A well-equipped machine shop could build without difficulty a *model machine* from detailed drawings, but the problem of matrix manufacture still had to be faced. The design and manufacture of the matrices invariably required a distinct and separate department in the manufactory.

Often the pioneering manufacturer's ability to produce a complete machine, including the matrices, was weakened by a lack of financial controls or knowhow, especially if the company was a small one. Substantial efforts were made to attract bond- or shareholders, yet huge amounts of money were lost or wasted through experimentation and the construction of trial machines. It is also apparent from some patent specifications that a number of inventors overlooked, perhaps ignored, the design and manufacture of their matrices, or they expected to use other inventors' styles, since they are not detailed in the patent specifications.

The plainest and simplest kind of matrix is the type founder's one-piece rectangular bar or block (Fig. 2.4) of brass or copper[5] into which the character is driven by a punch or engraved with the pantograph.

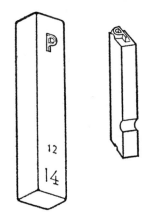

Fig. 2.4 Foundry matrix, with cast type. See Reference 15, p. 30.

Founders needed only one matrix for each character in a font,[6] whereas many thousands of matrices were required for composing machines. One could speculate that the type founder's style of matrix should have been a cue to a machine-inventor to keep his matrix simple and inexpensive. Yet some were complicated—they had a number of parts, or odd shapes, as shown in the illustrations. Matrix cost was a crucial financial consideration which could defeat a proposed machine even when it could be made to work satisfactorily in the workshop or experimental room.

The design of a machine dictated the configuration and movement of the matrix and, at times, the design of the matrix dictated the design of the machine. Some machines were designed to make and cast one letter with each stroke of the keyboard. With them, a movable rectangular matrix body could be used, such as Westcott's machine of 1871. But when matrices were to be assembled in contiguous lines, as foundry types were set in the composing stick, they had to be made with individual set-widths having very shallow sidewalls; when these sidewalls broke down from wear-and-tear, the result was "hairlines" between the letters, a drawback for which there has never been a satisfactory solution except replacement of the offending sorts. This was true whether the composable matrices were freely individual —as Mergenthaler's "Blower" matrices—or were captive ones, such as those which were arranged on long stems or arms that pivoted from central shafts and moved in arcs of circles to the mold. The basic difference between the one-stroke (pivoted) matrix and the individually composable matrix was this: one-stroke matrices were invariably retrograde captives, fixed in the machine, while

5. See drawing of a type founder's punch. (Fig. 1)

the individual (free) matrices, composable into castable lines, could be either retrograde or circulatory, but also removable from the machine for another font.[6]

Just as the earlier inventors of single-type setting machines were beset with difficulties, so also were the designers of matrix-using machines faced with seemingly insurmountable mechanical problems to work out. Legal complications sometimes entered the picture, usually involving the patent process. During the span of years discussed here (1885–1915), an inventor could not afford to wait for the expiration of another's patent—then a period of seventeen years—in order to adopt his matrix design, so he was forced to design his own style. To duplicate a matrix design could invite litigative charges of patent infringement. It was, however, possible to use an established matrix by not declaring it in the patent, but by giving credit to its origin, or naming the inventor.

In the same way that the early years of the nineteenth century saw a flurry of newly designed printing presses, the latter years were crowded with an oversupply of ideas for typesetting equipment. There were just too many unsuccessful proposals, and too many money-wasting efforts being made on all conceivable kinds of matrix-composing machines. A process of elimination and the inevitable expiration of patents eventually narrowed the field to three basic matrix-using systems which persist to this day, though severely restricted in use: the circulating matrix, the shiftable matrix, and the hand-set matrix.

The Plate Section in this book shows illustrations and advertisements of eight very different makes of composing machines: one patrix, and seven matrix. Of these eight only three achieved industry success: The *Monotype*, the *Linograph*, and the *Intertype*.

6. *Font*: a complete set of all the characters used in type composition; *sorts*: additional individual letters or characters needed to make up shortages.

V

STYLES OF HOT METAL MATRICES

All matrices may be classified into several basic groups or categories, each category having some interesting variations. (Although *patrices*[1] have not yet been fully explained, they are part of the overall picture of machine composition. Patrices are discussed in Chapter VIII and even this class has its variations and different applications.)

Matrices for machine composition could be used for casting types from hot metal[2] or *embossing*[3] on cold metal; regardless of the application, matrices could be circulatory or retrograde. A listing of the variations in matrices follows:

individual, circulating
individual, hand-set
individual, hand-shifted
individual, oscillating
individual, retrograde
individual, rotary
composite, matrix and mold combined
composite, plate form, square or round
composite, "monotype" cells in die-
    cases
composite, rotary or rotative
composite, oscillatory
composite, bar form
rotary, matrix and mold combined
tubular matrix sleeves

Within the composite bar form category, for instance a design by John Pearson (1905)[4] had the letters driven on four sides of short bars, several characters on each side. There

were only six bars in this machine, called the *Typobar*, yet altogether there was a full font of 100 matrix depressions. Each bar was rotatable over its own mold which cast single-types. The aperture in the Cade-Heldrich matrix head (1911, Fig. 3), served as a pas-

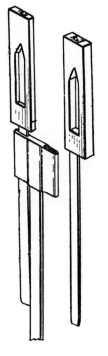

Fig. 3 Cade-Heldrich matrix. U. S. patent 1,035,416.

sageway for an aligning bar to slide through the composed line and straighten up the matrices prior to casting a slug, the die-sunk characters being in the ends of the heads.

Another inventor's style of matrix, for the Goodson *Graphotype* of 1893, was a rect-

1. *Patrices* are forms of "dies," and when engraved as metal punches will make deep impressions in various kinds of materials.
2. *Hot metal*: type metal melted in a crucible in the casting machine.
3. *Embossing*: this kind of matrix reversed the impression method by *raising* the printing-surface, similar in appearance to foundry type.
4. John R. Pearson built a one-man composing machine that used only six matrix-bars, square in section, each bar having different unit counts; the entire alphabet and miscellaneous characters were based on a 27-unit system.

angular plate into which the letters were arranged in rows. In other machines of this class, square or round plates were arranged similarly and all could easily be made by electrodepositing copper from a mold of a set-up foundry type alphabet (a form of pirating[5] founder's types); all of these plates were made for casting single-types.

Another style of matrix, used in the *Electrotypograph* (1897, Fig. 4), was arranged on the periphery of a wheel-like member or carrier, the letters being recessed into several flat surfaces for casting single-types. Or, several kinds of matrices were arranged on the ends of long rods, as in Charles Botz's 1897 machine (Fig. 5), a hand-operated slug caster. Another type caster, Franz Schimmel's *Rototype*, had its matrices on circulating matrix carriers in wheel form where ten flat surfaces contained the characters. One version of the *Rototype* (Fig. 6) for casting slugs appeared in 1907, another for casting single-types in 1909; both could use the same matrices.

Edmond Retaux's matrix of 1901 (Fig. 7) was one of the most unusual and most complicated of all, being "compound" with its own mold cell built into it and casting single-types in the form of a "comb." The type was later broken off the comb and pushed together to make a line.

Fritz Lucke's slug-casting *Polytype* (Plate II) of 1901 used a circulating matrix with a crescent-like shape (Fig. 8) containing up to five flat surfaces on the convex edge with as many characters. A surviving example of this machine is in the School of Journalism at the University of Missouri, Columbia.

The *Linotype Junior* matrices, 1901, were eight inches long (Fig. 9) with a hook at the top, casting slug-lines. This machine, incidentally, was *not* invented by Mergenthaler, as some erroneously think, but, in fact, was a derivative of the disbarred Rogers *Typo-*

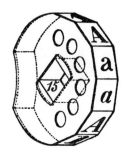

Fig. 4 Electrotypograph matrix. U. S. patent 765,059.

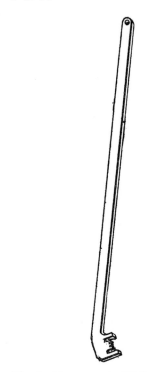

Fig. 5 Charles Botz matrix. U. S. patent 589,636.

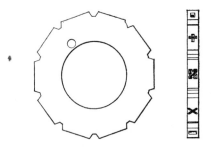

Fig. 6 Franz Schimmel's matrix. See Reference 7, p. 226.

5. This was a policy, for economic reasons, of "stealing" a design from another source.

graph, brought out after Mergenthaler's death, to compete with and eventually eliminate the few remaining single-type setters.

In a different category, A. W. Hanigan's 1907 matrix (Fig. 10), had twelve characters to a bar, each matrix-bar having a group of matrices of the same set-width, so that the number of set-widths (widths of letters) could be kept to a minimum and each bar-group worked against its own mold, casting single-types.

Several inventors of circulating-matrix machines designed *bifurcated*[6] matrices. These could be of two different styles. One had matrices with deep slots in their bodies extending upward from the bottom, thereby providing a means for carrying them in the machines by sliding them on wires or rails; the other style had a character driven into the bottom of a deep "well" on the casting edge of the matrix body, which in differing versions could serve as a full, or partial mold-cell for casting individual types. Another style of circulating matrix, used in the 1901 *Stringertype* (Fig. 11), resembled that of the *Linotype*, but here the letters were driven into the flat side. These matrices were presented to the mold[7] in rapid order one at a time, casting single-types, then returned to the assembling channel for distribution. These are only a few of the many styles of matrices developed so many years ago.

Several other inventors tried to develop slug-casting machines in which the matrices would slide in a side-by-side arrangement on a horizontal plane, the matrices being in long bar-form with partial, or full, alphabets on each bar. These sets of bars occupied a large amount of space on the table surfaces of the machines, were all captive, and varied in length from machine to machine. However, Erl Beals's sliding matrix bars of 1898 were short, carrying small groups of characters, and were tapered at both ends, permitting

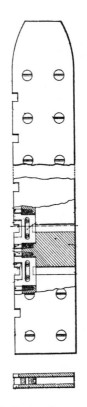

Fig. 7 Edmond Retaux's compound matrix. U. S. patent 919,951.

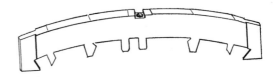

Fig. 8 Fritz Lucke's Polytype matrix. Drawing from matrix in author's possession.

them to pass each other as they moved back and forth while being aligned over a casting slot. Short types were cast from these matrix bars directly onto pre-cast one-line bases which were fed from a magazine in the machine, making what Beals called "composite type-bars." These matrix bars travelled only a short distance in either direction and remained in their "case."

6. *Bifurcated* means "divided into two branches, or forked."
7. The 1950 Intertype *Fotosetter* followed this principle, except the letters were photographed on negative or positive film, for offset printing.

In 1901, the Hungarian Zigmunt Halacinski took out a United States patent on a sliding-matrix machine (#694,269) designed to use long tapered bars containing full alphabets and points; the bars alternated directions in the machine and had to be aligned by hand *under* the mold for casting slugs in a face-down position.

Washington I. Ludlow's sliding matrices of 1907 (U. S. patent #856,539) were similar in principle to Halacinski's, having full alphabets and points on each bar. These bars were wedge-shaped, 24 inches long, with the thin characters in the thin ends and the widest characters in the thick ends; the bars alternated directions in the machine—several of which were actually built—moving in opposite directions to form matrix-lines over the mold from which slugs were cast face up. In this sliding-bar class, only Erl V. Beals's bar system had the advantage of interchangeable fonts, since the sliding matrix-bars were contained in a replaceable case. Both Halacinski's and Ludlow's bars were captive, built into the machines, limiting them to one kind and size of work, since they were integral parts of the machines. These inventors had the idea of supplying printers with small, cheap and easily-maintained machines at prices they could afford to pay, especially in "country towns." Also, because they were one-font machines, they could represent a costly problem for a printer who could have needed as many machines as type faces or sizes, the economics of which would have defeated the purpose of the inventors.

The class of machines using *circulating* individual matrices[8] followed a more-or-less similar principle and produced the most successful forms of composition, though there were as many different matrix configurations as there were inventors; some of these inventors even had developed alternate ver-

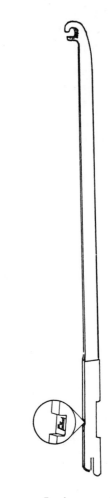

Fig. 9 Linotype Junior matrix. Drawing from matrix in author's possession.

sions of matrices for possible variations in their machines. Mergenthaler experimented with at least a dozen different patterns before he settled on the form of circulating matrix that has remained valid to this day. See Fig. 21 for the 1885 matrix, and the standard style of today.

8. In *circulation* the matrices passed from the magazine to the casting mechanism and then back to the magazine, repeating this continually. Fuller descriptions of matrix-using machines may be found in my book *The Development of Printers' Mechanical Typesetting Methods, 1822–1925.* See Reference 5.

Cold Metal Embossing Machines

Cold matrix composition in its truest and earliest form was developed in the 1880s and utilized a method for *embossing* characters instead of casting them. In this distinctive class of machines, the matrices were forced onto individual type-metal blanks, or onto blank line-bars by simple pressure or compression. Other designs called for the type metal elements to be driven into the matrices. Lanston's first "Monotype" machine, the 1887 *Embossing Type-Maker*, used cellular matrices which embossed the characters individually on the ends of single cold-metal blanks that were pre-cut from strips of type metal and dressed in the machine before presentation to the matrices.

In several different machines one letter at a time was embossed and assembled, while still others composed the entire line in matrices and then carried out the embossing action at one stroke. A good example of the latter is the St. John *Typobar* of 1890,[9] which used keyboard-composed *steel* matrices, the astronomical manufacturing cost of which helped to kill this powerful and ingenious machine.

Byron A. Brooks in 1887 patented a peculiar device intended to use a tubular *embossing "type barrel,"* having raised matrices on its periphery. The odd purpose here was to make "slugs" and then cut the words apart to serve as logotypes, which then had to be set up and justified by hand in the composing stick.

Several varieties of embossing machines used circulating matrices while others used retrograde matrices, sometimes restricting them to one kind and size of work. All too often these machines were cumbersome and too slow to be economically feasible. The difficulties in obtaining sharp, clean embossings could not be overcome in this class

Fig. 10 Hanigan's matrix bar. U. S. patent 896,908.

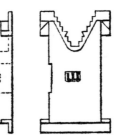

Fig. 11 Stringertype matrix. See Reference 7, p. 224.

of composing machines because of the resistance of cold metal to what was actually a form of cold molding. Under compression or concussion, extraneous metal had to go somewhere and the result was a "dirty" product—chips, flakes and small trimmings clut-

9. John S. Thompson, *History of Composing Machines*. Chicago: The Inland Printer Co., 1904, pp. 89–92. See Reference 20.

tered the finished lines, which were produced at too slow a rate anyway. The freedom inherent in flowing molten metal was absent. "Hot" was the answer, and "cold" just did not work out.

Electrotype Matrices

The subject of *electrotype matrices* was mentioned in a letter from a correspondent,[10] who asked if they would be included in this treatise. The reader may have noticed that this class of matrices has been scarcely mentioned so far because we are concerned principally with matrices made from punches and original or copied designs. But they *are* matrices, even though the practice of making them by the electrotype process was oftentimes a perfidious one. As the knowledgeable printer or historian is aware, many nineteenth century type founders were guilty of this unfair and annoying business practice in which they "stole" popular designs from one another. Intense competition, highlighted by the aggressive advertising campaigns mounted each time a "new" design was rushed out, was the goad which drove type founders to the unethical electrotyping of rival type faces; it was a cheap and convenient means of producing the individual matrices needed for type-casting machines, and was, moreover, totally unrestricted by the Copyright Office; ironically, many designs, even stolen ones, were claimed to be "patented." (In my research on the subject of composition matrices the only unofficial reference I have found on this practice is in *The Book of OZ Cooper* as noted in Chapter I.)

Using the electrotype method, there were, perhaps, allowable exceptions. The matrix plates for the Goodson *Graphotype* composer, for example, could be driven, engraved, or *electrotyped*, but Goodson recommended the electrotype process for making the plates as the least expensive, and therefore most attractive to the printer who had to bear the cost himself.

Individual composition matrices were necessarily small in size, especially those which circulated. Individual electrotype matrices simply were not adaptable to a circulating application, since their bodies had to be large enough to accommodate a single-cell adjustable mold designed to cast one size or face of type at a time, as in the Bruce and Barth foundry machines, or in the Monotype, Thompson, Universal and Bhisotype sorts casting machines, none of which were composing machines.

Historical references to the making of electrotype matrices are scattered and brief. Legros and Grant have only a few paragraphs on pages 238 and 239 of their *Typographical Printing-Surfaces*. Briefly, they state that "The easiest method . . . is by electrolytic deposition of copper. A type of the desired character can be surrounded by two pieces of type metal of a similar form to the mold . . . and the face of the matrix is thus obtained true . . . the rough deposited sides of the matrix are subsequently filed or machined true." Another process was to build up bearers around the type character (or group of characters) to be copied, make a wax mold as in regular electrotyping, then immerse the mold in an electrolytic bath until a sufficient shell of copper had been deposited. Further machining prepared the matrix for a proper fit in the type casting machine. Legros and Grant's experiments showed that "electrolytic copper is not generally hard enough to stand the wear."

Still another method of making this kind of matrix called for hand engravers to work on "soft metal" (probably type metal), cut-

10. Letter from Roy Rice, proprietor of The Recalcitrant Press and Typefoundry, Atlanta, Georgia.

1891 The method employed in this machine for the production of an equivalent of a Linotype slug appears, by present standards, to be somewhat indirect and slow. It required the combination into one machine of electromagnetic devices, controlled by a keyboard, for releasing specially formed type and type bars. These were assembled with double-wedge justifying spaces, the assembled type and spaces being held together by air blast. The line was justified and locked before and during impression into a blank to produce a matrix which was then carried and properly held against the face of a mold into which metal was cast to form a slug for printing.

To the mechanisms for performance of those functions, there were added mechanisms for packing the slugs onto a galley. Others were provided for supplying a new matrix blank for each new line, and for disposal of matrices after the cast was made, and still others for returning all parts to their normal positions ready for the next line of composition.

1891 · MATRIX
MAKING MACHINE

Plate I — From Milestones of Machine Typesetting

1911

This machine was the development of a line-casting machine invented about 1900. It employed special matrices, sections or segments of a ring of uniform thickness. Each matrix had on its outer convex surface, a plurality of dies for the same letter or sign in several faces, or even in several point sizes. On its inside concave edge were six teeth which not only held it to supports during composition, casting and transfer, but served also for distribution. The assembled line of matrices and spacers, of wedge design, was delivered onto either of two grooved supporting cylinders rotatively mounted on a large ring-shaped frame. This revolved on a horizontal axis to carry the cylinders to and through the positions of casting and transfer, and returned them to the assembling position. The grooved cylinders could be rotated to bring any desired line of the several type faces on the matrices into casting position.

The metal pot with its mechanism was inside, but not attached to, the large ring-shaped frame. An adjustable mold was moved horizontally to the left in order to locate it between the pot mouthpiece and the composed line on the grooved cylinder.

After the slug was cast, the mold was moved to the right and outside the ring-shaped frame to the ejecting position. During this movement the slug passed knives which trimmed its base and both edges of its face.

The keyboard, magazine and assembling mechanism resembled those of the Linotype, but a grooved roller was substituted for the assembling elevator. The distributor was somewhat like two of the earlier Mergenthaler distributors, set side by side. The machine was never used commercially.

Plate II – From Milestones of Machine Typesetting

Plate III – From The American Printer, 1905

THE MONOTYPE

Both Makes and Sets Type
The Only Type Caster and Composing Machine

Casts Type in All Sizes
5-point to 36-point
Body Type, Display Type
Borders, Spaces and Quads

For All Kinds of Composition
Plain or Intricate
All Sizes, 5-point to 14-point
Any Measure Up to 60 Picas

OUR TYPE CASTER [Con-vert-ible]

The Machine That Makes the Type Trust Peevish

Built on the unit system, Our Type Caster is adapted to the require-ments of either a large or a small printing office

The little fellow can use it for his own needs, and also can sell type to other printers. He can get a good price for this type too, for the Monotype Matrix Library gives him the choice of over 640 up-to-date fonts, and of course better type can not be made than Our Type Caster produces. Then when his office grows large enough, when he needs a composing machine, he can purchase the required units and convert his Type Caster (without lessening its efficiency for making type) into the most flexible and economical composing machine on the market—the Standard Monotype.

The big office, even if already equipped with composing machines, can use Our Type Caster at a profit, for it makes display type cheaper than it can be dis-tributed. It frees the printer from ex-tortionate type foundry bills. It elim-inates the time compositors lose picking and hunting for sorts. It improves the quality of the work. It reduces make-ready time to the minimum. Best of all, in purchasing Our Type Caster you have done more than install the most efficient màchine for its purpose ever made—you have paid more than half the cost of an additional composing machine.

Do not let the assertions of interested persons disturb your busi-ness judgment. Making your own type pays, and pays big, if you use the right machine. Let us send you samples of type made by Our Type Caster, together with conclusive proof of the money it would earn and the time it would save in your composing room.

LANSTON MONOTYPE MACHINE COMPANY
Philadelphia

Plate IV – From The Master Printer, 1910

The Linograph

Simple in Design
Made of Best Materials
Large in Capacity
Reasonable in Price
Two-Letter Equipment

Price
$1500

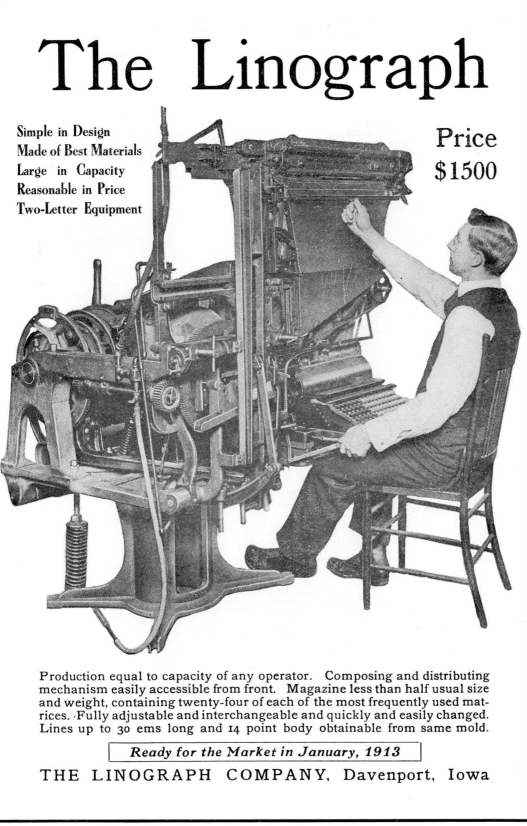

Production equal to capacity of any operator. Composing and distributing mechanism easily accessible from front. Magazine less than half usual size and weight, containing twenty-four of each of the most frequently used matrices. Fully adjustable and interchangeable and quickly and easily changed. Lines up to 30 ems long and 14 point body obtainable from same mold.

Ready for the Market in January, 1913

THE LINOGRAPH COMPANY, Davenport, Iowa

Plate V — From The American Printer, 1912

THE ROWOTYPE
A New Linecasting Machine for Printers and Publishers

The mechanisms incident to linecasting have been reduced in this the latest development in the printing art to the simplest and most accurate operation.

Substantially built and simple in operation. Operator need not be a machinist to successfully operate. Fonts are changed quickly. Simple typewriter keyboard.

This advertisement is our Announcement to the printing trade.

Full particulars will be supplied by addressing

THE OGDEN ROWOTYPE COMPANY
565 West Washington Boulevard, CHICAGO ILL.

Plate VI – From The Inland Printer, 1912

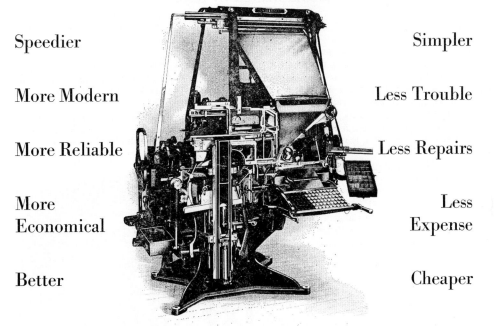
Plate VII — From The Printing Art, 1913

THE DISPLAYOTYPE

A New Typesetting Machine

That will do practically everything with type that is now being accomplished by hand

The DISPLAYOTYPE COMPOSING MACHINE is designed to be built along entirely different lines from composing machines now in use—the Displayotype will not be a competitor to the present machines, but is designed to go far beyond the present body type composing machines.

The Displayotype is designed to be a **DISPLAY** LETTER SLUG-CASTING MACHINE, and arranged so one machine may carry from **4 to 75 complete** fonts of DISPLAY TYPE MATRICES, ranging from 6 point extended to 120 point **face in depth, and** from 2 points to 216 points in width. This range will give regular, condensed and extended **faces in one machine.**

It will eliminate ALL distribution, **ALL cases,** case racks, sorts, etc. It will occupy LESS room than an ordinary double case rack. It will **eliminate ALL** wrong fonts and mixed cases—although several different sizes and faces may be used in the **same line at** the will of the compositor. It will eliminate the bother and loss of time of hunting for sorts, thin spaces, etc.

ALL COMPOSITORS will be OPERATORS, setting their own lines as occasion demands, with the aid of the machine instead of composing sticks, cases, etc.

It is a DISPLAY TYPESETTING MACHINE and is not to be classed as in competition with the present small letter composing machines.

This machine will be the greatest improvement in printing office equipment that has been brought out since the advent of typesetting devices, which are now so generally used in all large printing establishments for the composition of body matter of books and newspapers.

"I have known Mr. E. E. Wilson for fifteen years or more as a thoroughly practical printer, and am familiar with the idea he is developing. Such a machine will have a splendid market just as quickly as it is demonstrated to be what the designer claims."—*W. V. Cowgill, The Leader-News, Cleveland, O.*

"Your invention is right in the line of our normal necessities. It seems to me that you have gone Mr. Mergenthaler a point considerably beyond his accomplishment, up to date, in the setting of display type, and I hope that you may be able to perfect and place on the market a machine which will meet every-day requirements of a modern newspaper office."—*C. H. Fentress, The Cleveland Press.*

A rare opportunity for investors to acquire an interest in this wonderful machine. Get in on the ground floor and become an original subscriber to the capital stock of a $250,000 Stock Company now organizing. Send for literature giving complete information on this new machine, and investment particulars.

Address

E. E. Wilson

1514 Prospect Avenue

Cleveland, Ohio

The Displayotype (Patents applied for)

Plate VIII – From The Inland Printer, 1916

ting the original design to a suitable depth; from this engraving the matrix was built up in the electrolytic tank. This method had at least one distinct advantage over cutting steel punches, since very intricate designs could be engraved and reproduced in matrix form. William E. Loy's articles on "Designers and Engravers of Type" mention several craftsmen who worked on "soft metal," designing original faces for electrotyping instead of copying a brother-engraver's design.

The Inland Printer, Vol. 4 (March 1887) had a good illustrated article by Carl Schraubstadter, Jr., on how electrotype matrices were made. In this article, Edwin Starr, of Philadelphia, is given "the honor of a successful solution of the problem" and the article ends with this statement: "And lately Mr. Benton has cut Roman type on metal [soft metal] with his engraving machine, having such a high finish that it is safe to say that even in this field, until this time wholly given up to the punch cutter, the electrotype matrix will drive out its copper rival." These remarks, of course, refer to the type founders' "short-cut" methods of electrotyping matrices, exactly what Benton originally had in mind, but for his own foundry exclusively. He was not a punch cutter himself, but faced with the problem of replacing worn or "burned out" matrices, eventually perfected his justly famous engraving machine. At this point a new departure was made possible, a timely development, since the forthcoming matrices for composing machines had to be of a much tougher substance—brass, bronze, or even steel, which only Mergenthaler, it seems, had successfully attempted to produce.

VI

MATRIX MOVEMENTS

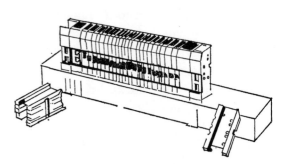

Fig. 12 Bellows Electric Compositor matrix. Drawing from photograph. See Reference 7, p. 233.

Many early matrix-composing machines were masterpieces of engineering skill and ingenuity, but a "masterpiece" and a practical, workable and economic machine were two different things. Besides their cost, the handling and *movement* of the matrices was of vital importance. The idea of a *free*[1] matrix was one of the great breakthroughs in this line of research, since free, or individually movable, matrices succeeded much more often than those of the *captive* class which were permanently part of their machines. Mergenthaler's *individual circulating matrices* were the first of this order to be developed, and are regarded as his most important contribution to hot metal composition. Other inventors might have originated similar systems, but were severely restricted by Mergenthaler's patents. Actually, there were few possibilities in this direction, since the circulating principle was unique and no one could improve on it. Only allowable, significantly different avenues could be explored, and only where a special or patent-free application was possible; indeed, variations from the Mergenthaler pattern were quite versatile.

Each of the following circulating styles had its own configuration and pattern of movement in their machines:

the *Rototype* (Fig. 6)
the *Polytype* (Fig. 8)
the *Linotype Junior* (Fig. 9)
the *Stringertype* (Fig. 11)
the *Bellows Electric Compositor*
    (Fig. 12)

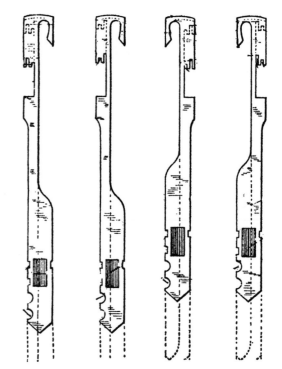

Fig. 13 Charles Forth Graphotype matrix. U. S. patent 562,954.

the *Forth* (Fig. 13)
the Mergenthaler-Lawrenz *Logotype Machine* (Fig. 14)
the *Grantype* (Fig. 15), for which two styles existed, one for single-types and one for sluglines.

1. The term *free* here denotes composable matrices that could easily be controlled in the machine, or removed from it and replaced by another font.

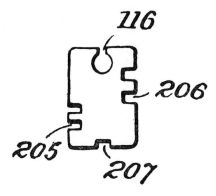

Fig. 14 Mergenthaler-Lawrenz Logotype matrix. U. S. patent 794,628.

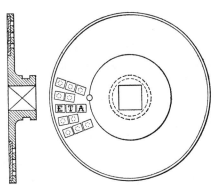

Fig. 16 Oddur matrix disc. See Reference 7, p. 226.

All of the circulating machines had matrices which could easily be corrected in the assembled lines before sending them to the casting mechanisms.

The *composite* matrices which took the form of square, rectangular or round plates contained whole fonts of characters and moved forward only a fraction of an inch to meet the mold, as in the Goodson *Graphotype*, or in the *Oddur* (Fig. 16). These plates presented only a small portion of their rigid surfaces to the mold cavity when the selected

"monotypes." Changing a font could be done in a short period of time by insertion of another plate or disc.

Circular matrix plates rotated, moved laterally when shifting from one ring of matrix depressions to another, and moved forward to meet the mold. Depending upon the machine, either full-height types or short types

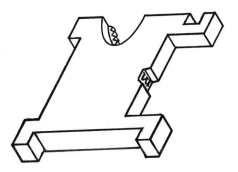

Fig. 15 Grantype matrix. See Reference 7, p. 225.

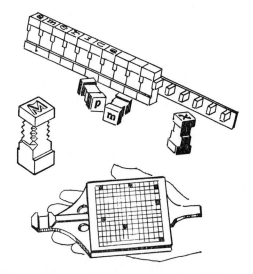

Fig. 17 Lanston Monotype matrix and die-case. See Reference 17, p. 9. Drawing from photograph.

matrix depression was in casting position, after having been shifted in two lateral directions in one version of the machine, or in two vertical directions in another version. In all cases they were controlled or manipulated by perforated tapes and cast

were cast from this class of matrices. Where short types were produced, they were either swaged or hooked to pre-formed metal bases to make them type-high, that is, .918″, also called "height-to-paper."

Matrices in the form of small *cells* were used in such machines as Tolbert Lanston's *Monotype*; and Frank A. Johnson's competing *Tachytype* of 1894. The matrix cells were single pieces held loosely in *die-cases* (Figs. 17, 17.1) that had the same movements as the plate matrices, but were more flexible in use than the plates since the cells were easily removable or re-arrangeable in the die-cases, according to the kinds and needs of the composition. Shifting movements in matrix-plate or die-case machines was a matter of only a few inches, which permitted them to be rather small.

Another kind of type-casting machine had matrices arranged on the *edges* of discs or rings, groups of which formed *drums* of varying widths and diameters (e.g. the *Dyo-type* of J. Pinel, 1908). The rings could be rotated together as a unit, or individually, and were selected by action of the keyboard mechanism, which moved them circumferentially or axially, as well as forward to make contact with the mold.

Some machines had oscillating matrices fixed on long stems or arms that traveled through an arc of as much as eighteen inches (e.g. *Rowotype*, 1912, Plate VI) between home position and the assembling or casting point; of these, several had another motion forward to meet the mold.

Circulating matrices followed several mechanical motions or routes through—or around—the machines, but all were based on keyboards as the starting points, the action of which released the matrices from the magazines by direct escapement or indirectly by magnets, switch-levers or relays. These matrices were sometimes delivered by gravity, others were removed from the magazines by direct mechanical or frictional means, and collected in assemblers or racks, sometimes called "sticks" by the inventors.

The *captive* category was wide-ranging, including some quite ingenious machines. The matrices in these machines were often restricted to a single size or face of type and such machines were used mainly in situations calling for one-measure typesetting—exploited mainly for reasons of economy—as in standard newspaper or cheap book composition.

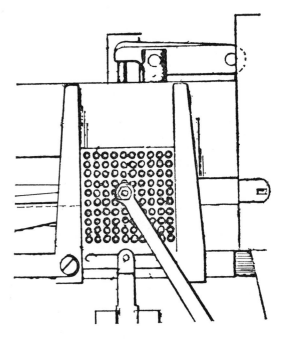

Fig. 17.1 Johnson's Tachytype matrix case. U. S. patent 548,365.

A few experimental captive-matrix machines were: Mergenthaler's Band Machine #2 of 1884, Gilbert-Stringer's Direct Caster of 1889, Kemp's machine of 1894, H. R. Rogers's *Typobar* caster of 1899, and the Cade-Heldrich slugcaster of 1911. In Mergenthaler's *Band Machine #2*[2] (Fig. 18) the matrices were long brass rods, or "bands,"

2. Several of these machines were built, but proved impractical and were abandoned; of the two surviving, one is in the Smithsonian Institution in Washington, but is inoperable, while the other is located at the School of Printing, Rochester Institute of Technology, and has recently been restored.

each having a series of characters driven into one edge; these bands were suspended side-by-side in the machine. Pressure on the keys released the bands to drop down to the assembling level, the desired letters being lined up at the casting slot by notches on the backs of the bands. If one letter became damaged the whole rod was useless—a serious drawback. This method, however, produced the original "line-o-type" slug, a description first used in 1886 by Whitelaw Reid when he saw the "Blower"[3] machine demonstrated in his composing room. (A visitor to the Smithsonian Institution in Washington can see one of the surviving Band Machines #2, as well as a fully restored "Blower" *Linotype*, now in operating condition. There is also a Band Machine #2 at the School of Printing, Rochester Institute of Technology). The retrograde[4] movement of these bar matrices, from the casting level back up to the storage level, was an inhibiting factor, and once convinced of this, Mergenthaler abandoned the idea.

Gilbert-Stringer's captive matrices were arranged on the face-edge of an arc of a cylinder, rotating and casting single-types. William Kemp's matrices were all fixed on the periphery of a wheel, and were designed to cast *short* types (Fig. 19) with a dove-tail on the bottom by which they were to be fastened to a base-plate with dove-tail grooves. H. R. Rogers's matrices were in circular segments mounted on a common shaft, with many segments making up a sort of revolving drum. The Cade-Heldrich matrix (Fig. 3) was on a long flexible stem, and oscillated in an upward direction to seat itself under the mold, located at the top of the machine.

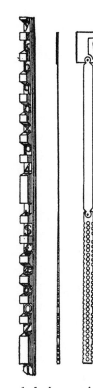

Fig. 18 Mergenthaler's matrix band. See Reference 7, p. 422.

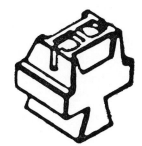

Fig. 19 Type made from William Kemp's wheel matrix. U. S. patent 540,059.

3. "Blower": this was a nickname given the first *Linotype* because the matrices were helped into the assembler by a blast of compressed air.
4. All retrograde (removing backward, or reversed) systems, except Lanston's *Monotype*, ultimately faded from the market.

VII

DISTRIBUTION OF MATRICES

Methods of *distributing* the matrices could be very complicated, or quite simple, depending on the design of the machine, and to a certain degree this applies to patrices. Circulating matrices all utilized some form of the *ward-and-key* principle,[1] each different character having its own set of combination nicks, hooks, lugs, teeth, recesses, holes, or shoulders; in certain cases even the length of the matrix-bars helped to distribute them. Mergenthaler's familiar V-cut with its small teeth set the pattern for most of the circulating styles, a pattern that hot-metal printers are familiar with to this day. The *Bellows* matrix, 1897 (Fig. 12), was rectangular, having combination holes in the side, into which feeler pins moved to make the proper channel selections; these matrices were first sorted and then sent into a "switching" mechanism similar in principle to that used in large railroad yards for routing freight cars onto many side-tracks.

Plate II shows Fritz Lucke's *Polytype* machine of 1901, the matrices of which (Fig. 8) had sets of teeth and lugs, both of which were used to assemble and to distribute these matrices. After being raised to the top of the machine by a grooved roller, where a single screw moved them along to their drop-off points, the matrices were returned to their appropriate magazine channels by means of combination teeth on the inside of the curved matrix carrier.

Charles Forth's matrices, 1892 (Fig. 13), used both graduated shoulders and "eyes" of varying sizes, and the length of the matrix-

bars helped in distribution. These matrices could be in either two-letter or three-letter form, first being separated into right and left groups by eight lengths, then passed onto "pick-up" rails which sorted them by the difference in their shoulder combinations, then dropped onto the individual rails. Slugs were cast from the assembled matrices in a separate machine, the lines being held in a form of "stick." After casting, this "stick" was returned to the composer for distribution.

The Mergenthaler-Lawrenz *Logotype* matrix, 1901 (Fig. 14), was a smooth, flat rectangle of brass with rounded corners that had milled-out notches on one side which first passed over feelers for selection into one of eight groups before moving into the distributor where a second set of feelers entered notches on the opposite side and directed it to its proper destination in the magazine. These matrices were assembled into words or parts of words and used to cast *logotypes*[2] with automatically calculated spaces cast on the ends of the words; the logotypes in turn were assembled to form the text matter being set. It was an extremely complicated machine, that can be seen on display in the Henry Ford Museum at Dearborn, Michigan.

Non-circulating (retrograde) matrices were available in a large variety of machines. Those fastened to central or common shafts, as in the Botz type-caster (Fig. 5), or those pivoted in concentric arcs of circles, used the simplest distribution principle of all—once a line was composed, a swinging

1. The ward and key principle is very old. It is most commonly exemplified in any padlock using a key having a variably cut serrated edge. The serrations or notches must correspond with mating plates or tumblers within the lock, pushing them back or aside a sufficient distance to permit the lock to be opened.
2. *Logotypes*: two or more letters cast in one piece—supposed to be a time-saver.

movement to home position concluded the movement of the matrices (observe the action of the type-bars in a typewriter). This method had a serious drawback in that the operator had to wait until the line of type was cast and the matrices were distributed before he could start the next line. Other retrograde methods using matrix-bars with several characters on each bar employed a sliding motion, in either horizontal or vertical directions. In one such machine (Wilbur Scudder's 1892 *Monoline*) the bars were dropped from the magazine into the assembler—only a short distance—and then, after the slug was cast, were pulled back into the magazine by wires or hooks.

Many classes of retrograde matrices did not "distribute" at all; for instance, the composite-plate or die-case styles moved in horizontal or vertical directions (at right angles) before making the cast; after the advancement to the mold they retracted (the retrograde movement) to release the type-heads allowing the mold to be opened for ejection of the types. Composite matrices in the form of round plates, except for their rotating motion, had the same retrograde movement as the square-plate and die-case styles. Finally, *rotary* matrices simply continued to turn on their axes after casting the types until they were again in starting position, where they remained until called for again by the keyboard.

VIII

PATRIX METHODS

A large number of inventors took a radically different approach to the manufacture of sluglines, and of stereotype[1] or electrotype[2] *page molds*. Utilizing *patrices*, the class of composing machines they designed may be described as *matrix-makers* and is based on a concept much older than that upon which matrix-using machines are based. It, therefore, must be regarded as a major category and can be sub-divided into the following groups:

> individual, circulating
> individual, oscillating
> individual, retrograde
> composite, bar form
> composite, sliding
> rotary
> type wheel, or type ring
> type-sleeve.

Throughout the period from 1843 to 1925, patrix methods were employed for four different purposes: a) the striking and casting of single-types in line form; b) the casting of solid sluglines; c) the impression of whole page or column matrices for stereotype or electrotype casting; and d) direct printing—some of the machines in this last group were adaptable to both cold-impression matrix-making (stereotyping) and pre-printing ("cold-type") methods.

A *patrix*—the opposite of matrix, in that it was in relief, as a punch—was used to make intaglio impressions on such soft molding materials as stereotyper's board, papier-mâché, type-metal blanks, strips of end-grain wood,

specially-prepared clay, or gutta-percha. The stereotype matrix resulting from this method might be in single-line form for casting sluglines, or in "sheet" form for casting whole pages or columns. Some inventors attempted to use founders' types as punches, but they soon wore out and had to be replaced. Patrices generally were made of brass, bronze, or steel.

Single-stroke *one-line* matrix-making machines drove the patrices one at a time into the molding material which moved in incremental distances based on the set-width of the patrices. In this class of impression machines the finished *one-line matrix* was presented to a mold, sometimes in the composing machine and sometimes in a separate casting machine; as soon as a slug was cast, the line-matrix was discarded and replaced by another as the slug was delivered to the galley. The 1896 Lee and LeBrun machine composed and impressed whole lines at one stroke (Fig. 20), discarding the line matrices immediately afterwards. An example of this machine is now in the Henry Ford Museum, Dearborn, Michigan.

Full-page or column-style machines either struck one letter at a time into the matrix material, or first composed a line of patrices and then struck them all at once into the material. This was a continuous operation, line after line, until the whole page or column had been composed and impressed. Whole-page matrices were then ready to go to the stereotyper or the electrotyper.[3] One must

---

1. *Stereotype*: a whole page cast from an impressed page mold. This mold or "mat" was placed in a "casting box" and molten type metal poured in to form a solid plate for printing.
2. *Electrotype*: a composed page of type was molded in "wax" or soft lead, which was treated to receive a coating of copper in an electrolytic tank; this made a "shell" of copper upon the back of which type metal was poured, forming a "duplicate" printing plate known as a "copperplate."
3. A number of impression machines were hand operated, mainly by turning a disc or wheel containing

wonder about the difficulties of proofreading —and correcting—this means of composition.

The inventors of these devices invariably worked on the supposition that hand-set types could be eliminated. Although a few inventors succeeded in building machines that could impress stereotype molds, they could never overcome the difficulties inherent in the method, and base a successful enterprise on their equipment. Mergenthaler himself experimented with impression devices in the early years of his typographic career. His Rotary Indenting Machine of 1883 worked after a fashion, but was a failure so far as the papier-mâché matrix was concerned. Next was the cleverly engineered Bar Indenting Machine of 1884, also known as Band Machine #1, a device which used long bars with raised characters along one edge. This too was a failure and for the same reason as the Rotary Machine—good papier-mâché matrices were impossible to achieve. This machine may be seen in the Henry Ford Museum.

A vexing problem for all versions of cold-impression machines—matrix or patrix—was the displacement of metal or other material when a die or punch hit the surface of whatever base or blank material was in a particular machine. Unless allowances were made in the blank material before the impression was made, a peening or "flow" effect of material resulted around the area of impact, as it was forced out in all directions. The flowage created a bulge around the area of each letter which had to be eliminated by compression or by trimming. The crowding and distortion of adjacent letters and the maintainance of an accurate and uniform depth of impres-

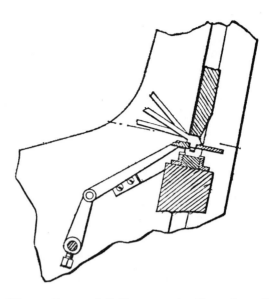

Fig. 20 Lee and LeBrun patrix die and anvil head. U. S. patent 551,469.

sion for each letter or line struck were particularly troublesome shortcomings, and the principal reason impression machines failed.

Regarding the design and manufacture of patrices, unfortunately almost no details can be offered here. When patrix- or male-die machines were mentioned in trade journal announcements it seems to have been taken for granted that their patrices were to be made by methods similar but in reverse to those for making matrices. W. E. Loy in his twenty-seventh article on "Designers and Engravers of Type" identifies Henry Schuneman as the engraver of steel letters for the first model of the *Rogers Typograph*, an impression machinge using patrices. These were actually combination brass-steel patrix plates, which were designed to slide down the wires in an elliptical frame into the assembler. After the line had been impressed, the operator tipped the frame backwards and the patrices returned to home position by gravity. This machine was a "flop" and soon replaced by the hot-metal machine of 1890 bearing the same name, but using matrices.

the dies, or punches; plungers drove them into the matrix material. The first such patent in the United States was No. 20,081, granted to John McElheran in 1858.

In their great work *Typographical Print-ing-Surfaces*, Legros and Grant are totally silent on his class of patrices, which is a pity. Evidently they were manufactured by different methods, for patrices had to be "wrong-reading" in order to make a "right-reading" impression in the matrix material, just as the founders' punches were in reverse in order to make foundry matrices. Then too, the patrices had to be made of a hard alloy, and could have been formed by pantographic engraving, by an indirect impression method, or by die-casting, but above all they had to be very durable. Simply put, they performed the same function that punches did when making type matrices.

Patrix technology was also employed for the *direct printing*, or "typing" of copy, that was later prepared for transfer to flat plates or litho stones. The foregoing is now called "strike on[4] typesetting" for offset printing and is used in electric typewriters. One can only smile at how old the "modern" ideas are.[5]

Three early examples of this use of the patrix—or, in a typewriter, the type bar—are discussed here: In 1902, Charles Sears of Cleveland brought out his *Sears Direct Print-er*, which, oddly, prepared copy for transfer to sensitized metal plates, the end result—after etching—being a *relief* plate for letterpress printing, instead of the usual lithographic direct plate. W. S. Timmis's *Litho-type* of 1903 used a type sleeve which printed on transfer paper, and after page make-up, was printed on a flat litho plate in a transfer press. These litho plates were usually made of zinc, which replaced the older litho stones

in some establishments, where, it should be noted, flatbed presses were used.[6] Rotary off-set printing on paper as understood today had not yet been developed, though by 1904 Ira W. Rubel and Alexander Sherwood had nearly perfected the process.[7]

The third machine in the direct printer class was the *Typary*, which originated in Switzerland in 1924, and was extensively advertised in the United States. This was a massive machine with a standard typewriter keyboard and type-bars 3⅝ inches long, that shifted back and forth when making their prints on a roll of photosensitive paper. The paper was then developed to make a negative, or positive, film for offset plate making.

---

4. *Direct printing*: these machines could be said to work like typewriters, but were sometimes automated in that they were controlled by perforated paper tapes, and "printed" directly on paper or other suitable material, later to be transferred to the lithographic stone; they were not typewriters in the usual sense.

5. Richard E Huss, "Development of Typewriters for Printers' Composition," in *The Printer*, Findlay, Ohio (October 1975), p. 3; now defunct.

6. The following comment on Ira Rubel was offered in a personal letter by Dr. James Eckman, a printing historian in Rochester, Minnesota: "His contributions to the . . . application of offset lithography are largely fanciful. Offset lithography had been in use in the United States for 25 years in the metal decorating industry before Rubels' first offset lithography press was built. . . . Robert Barclay's patent on his offset lithography press was granted in 1875. . . . R. Hoe & Company built an offset lithography press for metal decorating in 1889, and . . . such presses had been imported from Europe before that year. Rubel, a lawyer, probably saw one and then simply substituted a sheet of paper for a sheet of metal, and thus was given credit for a process that was clearly derivative."

7. *Metal Decorating From Start to Finishes*, by Charles R. Bragdon, is quite lucid on the history of metal decorating by the "offset" method. Published by The Bond Wheelwright Company, Freeport, Maine, 1961. See Reference 2.

IX

THE ULTIMATE THREE STYLES
OF MATRICES

Many different styles of matrices and patrices were designed and manufactured during the innovative early years of machine-matrix composition, but none were interchangeable between different machines. There was too much individuality among inventors and too much competition between composing machine businesses to permit this. Not until after Mergenthaler's patents ran out did interchangeability become possible. The standards had clearly been set by the Linotype matrices, though after 1912 the Linotype monopoly was broken and a number of other "slug" casting systems were exploited vigorously in America and Europe.

As with developments in many other fields of industry during the nineteenth century, including the invention of the reaper and the harvester, the telegraph, the telephone, steam locomotion for railway and ocean travel, the typewriter, and even the automobile, the art of mechanical typesetting by using matrices grew apace toward the end of the century; individuality largely became lost in the great maze of modifications, ramifications and combinations. Inventions became merged into a few systems, and these systems were swallowed up by pragmatic companies. Consequently, the long and financially painful process of elimination reduced a wide variety of matrix-composing methods to just *three basic systems* as typified in the *Linotype*, the *Monotype*, and the *Ludlow*.

In its final form, Mergenthaler's circulat-

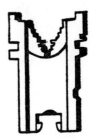

Fig. 21 Mergenthaler "Blower" matrix. See Reference 21, p. 150.

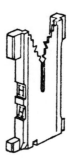

Fig. 21.1 Present-day Mergenthaler matrix. Any Linotype literature.

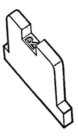

Fig. 22 Ludlow Typograph matrix. Any Ludlow literature.

ing matrix[1] (Figs. 21, 21.1) became the standard pattern for every subsequent make of keyboard-operated slug-casting machine. Lanston's matrix-cell principle (Fig. 17)

1. Mergenthaler experimented with about a dozen different kinds of matrices until he arrived at a matrix similar to today's Linotype matrix. See Reference 11. Mergenthaler's most important contribution to mechanical typesetting was perfecting the principle of automatic circulation of individual matrices in his machine.

was imitated but never bettered, and remains to this day the only survivor in its class. William A. Reade's 1911 system of hand-set matrices, manufactured and sold under the name of *Ludlow* (Fig. 22), is still a valuable adjunct to hot-metal display composition. The *All-Purpose Linotype* (APL) of the 1930s borrowed the Ludlow principle, but the heavy, complicated machine soon faded from the marketplace; The Whittaker S·A·M (for Suits All Matrices) machine was a British version manufactured in the 1950s, while the more recent *Nebitype* is an Italian version made in the 1960s and 1970s. Ex-

cepting typewriters, no *patrix-using machine ever achieved economic success*.

In the 1980s the almost universal use of computers and photocomposers for the composition of reading matter seems to have sounded the death knell for hot-metal type composition. Notwithstanding this embrace of modern technology, the esthetics of letterpress printing are still promulgated by a small but bravely enthusiastic segment of the great printing industry. The sharp, clear, three-dimensional effect achieved with metal type can not be surpassed by any other printing method.

APPENDICES

The Appendices list the names of inventors, and their machines when known, in chronological order. After patenting their *original* inventions many inventors continued to make improvements in their machines, or re-design them, which they also patented, and this accounts for the repetitions in the names. The fact that these machines are so thoroughly documented in the official patent records shows that there was a very active group of men attempting to provide printers with a mechanical means for setting types. A total of 59 patrix machines are listed which were patented between 1843 and 1925, and 107 matrix machines are listed between 1843 and 1925. Sources of information are indicated by the following key letters:

AS = Antoine Seyl, *La Composition Mécanique.* Bruxelles: Imprimerie Scientifique et Littéraire, 1926.

ADP = *American Dictionary of Printing and Bookmaking.* New York: H. Lockwood & Co., 1894.

BPO = British Patent Office. London.

COS = Carl Otto Schoenrich, *Biography of Ottmar Mergenthaler and History of the Linotype, Its Invention and Development.* Baltimore: The Friedenwald Company, 1898.

FMS = Frank M. Sherman, *The Genesis of Machine Typesetting.* Chicago: M & L Typesetting and Electrotyping Co., 1950.

INT = The Intertype Company, *The Development of the Intertype.* Boston: 1937.

IP = *The Inland Printer.* Chicago, Illinois.

JM = James Moran, *The Composition of Reading Matter.* London: Wace & Co., 1965.

JST = John S. Thompson, *History of Composing Machines.* Chicago: The Inland Printer Co., 1904.

LG = Legros and Grant, *Typographical Printing-Surfaces.* London: Longmans, Green and Co., 1916.

MS = *Milestones of Machine Typesetting.* Brooklyn: Mergenthaler Linotype Co., 1944.

OH = Otto Höhne, *Geschichte der Setzmaschinen.* Leipzig: Der Deutschen Buchdrucker G.M.B.H., 1925.

REH = Richard E Huss, *The Development of Printers' Mechanical Typesetting Methods, 1822–1925.* Charlottesville, Va., The University Press of Virginia, 1973. Also *Dr. Church's "Hoax".* Willow Street, Pa.: Graphic Crafts, Inc., 1976.

ScA = *Scientific American.*

USP = United States Patent Office.

APPENDIX A

PATRIX COMPOSING MACHINES

An asterisk (*) indicates machines known to have been built, though some were only patent demonstration models.

1843 — Joseph Mazzini—*Uniplane*. BPO, patent 1843–9731.

1844 — J. V. Gallien and C. Armangaud—*Coptotype*. AS, pp. 70, 71.

1853 — John Jones—*Typographer**. ScA, May 7, 1853.

1854 — R. S. Thomas—*Typographer**. REH, p. 45.

1856 — Joseph Marzolo—*Melodian*. BPO, patent 1856–145.

1858 — John McElheran—*Spoke-Disc Impresser*. USP, patent 20,081.

1859 — D. Brainard Ray—*Stereo-Bar*. USP, patent 24,662.

1864 — F. A. DeMey—*Typographer**. REH, p. 59.

1864 — J. D. McLean—*Stereotype Mold Machine*. USP, patent 43,323.

1866 — Pierre Flamm*. USP, patent 59,522.

1866 — John Paulding. USP, patent 52,073.

1867 — John McNair, USP, patent 72,515.

1867 — Mortimer Nelson. USP, patent 65,501.

1867 — John E. Sweet*. REH, p. 66.

1871 — Alexander Shiland. USP, patent 119,537.

1872 — Merritt Gally—*Stereo Telegraph #1*. USP, patent 119,537; IP, Nov. 1902, p. 212.

1872 — Merritt Gally—*Stereo Telegraph #2*. USP, patent 129,331.

1879 — Ole M. Peterson—*Impression Typesetter*. REH, p. 92.

1879 — Jacobs W. Schuckers—*Cold Impression Machine*. REH, p. 133; USP, patent 222,642.

1880 — M. H. Dement. REH, p. 104.

1880 — Robert L. Kimberley. USP, patent 227,017.

1883 — Ottmar Mergenthaler—*Rotary Matrix Machine**. FMS, p. 14.

1883 — Ottmar Mergenthaler—*Band Machine #1**. COS, pp. 11, 12.

1887 — George G. Allen—*Typesetter-Printer*. REH, p. 122.

1888 — A. S. Capehart—*Electro-Matrix**. ADP, p. 157.

1889 — V. F. Lake and Isaac Risley—*Transfer Composing Machine**. IP, March 1889.

1889 — Turbelin. AS, p. 73.

1890 — A. J. Kletzger and J. G. Goesel—*Impression Machine**. JST, p. 92.

1890 — John R. Rogers—*Impression Typograph**. REH, p. 134.

1890 — Charles L. Travis—*Electro-Matrix Impresser*. REH, p. 132.

1891 — George Calder—*Matrix, Machine*. USP 444,124.

1891 — George Calder—*Matrix Machine #4*. USP 444,125.

1891 — Homer Lee and Edmond LeBrun—*Matrix-Making Machine**. MS, p. 8.

1892 — T. T. Heath—*Matrix Typograph**. JST, pp. 96–98.

1892 — Caspar Redfield—*Matrix Maker*. USP 468,973.
1892 — Caspar Redfield—*Matrix Maker*. USP 468,974.
1892 — Caspar Redfield—*Typo-Matrix Maker*. USP 468,975.
1892 — Charles Sears—*Typo-Matrix**. JST, p. 96.
1892 — Henry A. Stall—*Stall's Linotype*. REH, p. 152.
1892 — Frank A. Johnson—*Tachytype Impression Machine*. REH, pp. 152, 153.
1896 — Charles E. Allen—*Stenotype*. IP, August 1896.
1896 — C. Meráy Horváth and C. Rozár—*Electric Stereo Typograph**. IP, October 1896.
1897 — Ole M. Peterson and C. C. Hill—*Impression Matrix Maker*. IP, March 1897.
1898 — Frank A. Johnson—*Tachytype**. IP, November 1898.
1899 — Philip T. Dodge—*Impression Linotype*. USP 618,044.
1900 — Isaac Risley—*Stereotype Composer*. REH, p. 209.
1901 — Henri C. Van Hoyweghen—*Stéréographe**. IP, January 1901, p. 636.
1902 — Alfred Kraus and Norman Collins—*Matrix-Maker*. REH, p. 224.
1902 — Charles T. Moore—*Planeograph**. JST, p. 136.
1902 — Charles Sears—*Direct Printer**. IP, October 1903.
1902 — W. S. Timmis—*Lithotype**. IP, April 1904.
1906 — John D. Morgan—*Planographic Composer*. USP, patent 1,056,042.
1907 — Byron A. Brooks—*Bandotype*. USP, patent 964,205.
1908 — Giovanni Novi—*Matrix Maker*. USP, patent 1,100,145.
1909 — F. H. Brown, J. L. Sellar—*Brohansel Planographic Machine**. USP, patent 921,946.
1910 — Heinrich Degener—*Combination Machine*. REH, p. 259.
1913 — John D. Morgan. USP, patent 1,056,042.
1924 — Polygraph Company—*Typary**. IP, September 1925.
1925 — Antoine Seyl—*Typostéreotype*. AS, pp. 76–80.

APPENDIX B

MATRIX COMPOSING MACHINES

Matrix Composing Machines. An asterisk (*) indicates machines known to have been built, some of which were patent demonstration models.

1843 — Joseph Mazzini—*Uniplane*. REH, p. 33; BPO, 1843–9731.

1870 — W. S. Shipley—*Air-blast Typesetter*. USP, 110,077.

1871 — Charles Westcott*, JST, p. 70; REH, p. 72.

1882 — Joseph Liwczak—*Threaded-type Machine*. BPO, 1882–1316; REH, p. 101.

1885 — Ottmar Mergenthaler—*Band Machine #2*. MS, p. 4; REH, p. 115.

1885 — Ottmar Mergenthaler—*"Blower" Linotype*. ScA, March 9, 1889; REH, p. 117.

1886 — Ernst Wentscher. JST, "Composing Machines, Past and Present," IP, October 1903, p. 36; REH, p. 122.

1887 — Byron A. Brooks—*Logotype Caster*. IP, December 1899; USP, 635,649.

1887 — Tolbert Lanston—*Embossing Typemaker*. IP, May 1924; REH, p. 124.

1889 — Ottmar Mergenthaler—*Square Base Linotype*. ScA, August 8, 1890; REH, p. 130.

1890 — R. H. St. John—*Typobar*. IP, June 1903; REH, 135.

1890 — Tolbert Lanston-*Triangle Monotype*. REH, p. 139.

1890 — Ottmar Mergenthaler—*Simplex Linotype*. ScA, January 13, 1894; REH, pp. 136, 137.

1890 — John R. Rogers—*Typograph*. REH, p. 133.

1890 — Wilbur Scudder—*Curved Slug Caster*. REH, p. 136; USP 444,090.

1891 — Tolbert Lanston—*2d Hot Metal Machine*. IP, May 1924; REH, p. 142.

1892 — Charles Forth—*Matrix Assembler*. USP, 562,954.

1892 — Joseph C. Fowler—*Type Bar Machine*. USP, 481,920.

1982 — Joseph C. Fowler—*Castotype*. JST, p. 74; REH, p. 222.

1892 — Isaac McKim Chase—*Expandable Type Bar*. USP, 490,793.

1892 — Jacobs W. Schuckers. USP, 474,306.

1892 — Wilbur Scudder—*Monoline*. IP, July 1901.

1893 — Victor Calendoli—*Calendoli*. ScA, April 6, 1895.

1893 — S. D. Carpenter—*Logo-Typer*. IP, August 1893.

1893 — George A. Goodson—*Graphotype*. IP, October 1900.

1893 — Tolbert Lanston—*Angle-end Monotype*. FMS, p. 42.

1893 — Tolbert Lanston—*Four-Tower Monotype*. FMS, p. 43.

1894 — Charles Forth—*Matrix Assembler*. USP, 562,816.

1894 — Joseph C. Fowler—*Direct Caster*. REH, p. 166.

1894 — William Kemp—*Type Bar*. USP, 540,743.

1894 — Frank A. Johnson—*Tachytype**. REH, p. 169.

1895 — Lucien A. Brott—*Composite Type Bar**. IP, October 1903.

1896 — William Berri—*Caster-Composer*. USP, 614,340.

1896 — Darien W. Dodson—*Type Bar Maker*. REH, p. 177.

1897 — Benjamin F. Bellows—*Electric Compositor**. IP, March 1903, p. 900.

1897 — Charles J. Botz, REH, p. 182.

1897 — C. Meráy Horváth and C. Rozár—*Electrotypograph**. IP, September 1903.

1898 — Erl V. Beals—*Printing-Bar Machine*. REH, pp. 189, 190.

1898 — H. J. S. Gilbert-Stringer—*Direct Caster*. REH, p. 197.

1898 — Carl Muehleisen—*Round-base Linotype**. FMS, p. 12; REH, pp. 194, 195.

1898 — Carl Muehleisen—*Twin Linotype**. IP, July 1903.

1898 — M. W. Smith—*Caster-Composer*. IP, May 1900, p. 209.

1899 — Ottmar Mergenthaler—*8-Character Linotype*. IP, January 1899.

1899 — H. R. Rogers—*Type Bar Caster*. USP 405,273.

1900 — *Canadian-American Linotype**. IP, July 1902; REH, pp. 206, 207.

1900 — John Sellers Bancroft—*Monotype**. IP, September 1903.

1900 — H. J. S. Gilbert-Stringer—*Stringertype**. LG, pp. 415–420; REH, p. 211.

1900 — Carl Schleicher. OH, p. 235.

1900 — Oddur V. Sigurdsson—*Oddur Type-Bar**. LG, pp. 464.

1901 — Herbert E. Brown—*Bar-O-Type**. IP, July 1914; REH, p. 213.

1901 — Philip T. Dodge—*Linotype Junior**. IP, August 1908.

1901 — Zigmunt Halacinski, USP 694,269.

1901 — Fritz P. Lucke—*Polytype**. MS, p. 15; REH, p. 220.

1901 — Ottmar Mergenthaler and Emil Lawrenz—*Logotype Machine**. MS, p. 13; REH, pp. 217–219.

1901 — Edmond Retaux—*Compound Matrix Caster*. REH, p. 221.

1901 — John R. Rogers—*Linotype*, USP, 678,036.

1901 — Alfred W. Storm—*Electric Linotype*. USP, 660,263.

1902 — Joseph C. Fowler—*Castotype**. JST, pp. 74, 75.

1902 — Joseph Pinel—*Dyotype**. USP, 890,706.

1902 — Francis H. Richards—*Type Bar*. REH, p. 231.

1903 — J. R. Dougall, D. A. Poe, W. H. Scharf—*Baby Linotype**. REH, p. 227.

1904 — Shanker A. Bhisey—*Triform Composer*. LG, p. 606.

1904 — Byron A. Brooks*. JST, p. 75.

1904 — Thomas A. Houghton. USP, 777,855.

1905 — Shanker A. Bhisey—*Triform Composer*. USP, 789,708.

1905 — Philip T. Dodge—*Logotype Machine*. REH, p. 234.

1905 — Edward A. Osse. USP, 778,996.

1905 — John R. Pearson and Gustave R. Pearson—*Typobar**. IP, February 1906.

1905 — John R. Rogers—*Logotype Machine*. USP, 804,050.

1905 — Franz Schimmel—*Rototype**. JM, pp. 50, 51.

1905 — John S. Thompson—*Caster-Composer*. USP, 1,719,769.

1906 — Fred E. Bright—*Bright-Type*. USP, 832,769.

1906 — John R. Rogers—*Caster-Composer*. USP, 883,425.

1906 — Ludwig Schmidt. USP, 843,304.

1906 — Washington I. Ludlow—*Typograph**. FMS, p. 30; REH, p. 238.

1907 — W. Ackerman and W. Nichols—*Graphotype**. LG, pp. 408–413.

1907 — A. W. Hanigan—*Type Bar*. REH, p. 241.

1907 — William E. Brand—*Monoman*. REH, p. 243.

1907 — Otto Koske. REH, p. 242.

1907 — David Petri-Palmedo—*Logotype Machine*. USP, 848,318.

1907 — Ludwig Schmidt, USP, 843,304.

1908 — Shanker A. Bhisey—*Bhisotype**. LG, p. 247.

1908 — Otto Koske. USP, 941,932.

1908 — John R. Rogers—*4-Bar Type Caster*. USP, 883,425.

1908 — Oddur V. Sigurdsson—*Cylinder Type Caster*. USP, 889,820.

1909 — Tadeusz Dropiowski—*Unit Caster*. BP, 1909–26,375.

1909 — John C. Grant—*Grantype**. LG, pp. 450–452.

1909 — Rolls P. Link—*Unitype-Bar**. USP, 979,864.

1909 — William A. Reade—*Ludlow Typograph**. REH, p. 254.

1909 — Franz Schimmel—Rototype*. REH, p. 257.

1910 — Byron A. Brooks—*Bandotype*. USP, 964,205.

1910 — Heinrich Degner—*Victorline**. LG, pp. 436, 437.

1910 — Philip T. Dodge—*Sorts Inserter*. USP, 1,055,388.

1911 — E. E. Barber—*Amalgatype**. REH, p. 263.

1911 — Baylus Cade and Andrew Heldrich—*Linecaster*. USP, 1,035,416.

1912 — Alfred C. Hatch—*Rowotype**. IP, October 1912.

1912 — G. Ray Horton and D. G. Holt—*Castaline**. AS, pp. 117, 118.

1912 — Hans Pedersen—*Linograph**. IP, July 1913; LG, p. 437.

1912 — Hugo Scholtz. REH, p. 274; BP, patent 1912–14,094.

1913 — International Typesetting Machine Company—*Intertype**. REH, p. 277; INT, H. R. Freund, *The Development of the Intertype*, Boston 1937.

1914 — Herbert E. Brown—*Bar-O-Type**. IP, July 1914; JST, pp. 117–119.

1914 — John S. Thompson. USP, 1,119,769.

1916 — E. E. Wilson—*Displayotype**. IP, October 1916.

1917 — Baylus Cade—*Comptotype*. Source lost.

1921 — A. F. Österlind and F. C. Damm—*Typocrat**. IP, March 1922, p. 90.

1922 — Frederick A. Letsch—*Supertype**. JM, p. 59; IP, May 1923, p. 244.

1925 — David Petri-Palmeda—*Standard Compositor**. IP, August 1925, p. 782.

AFTERWORD

Since machine typesetting had its genesis in the inventions of Dr. William Church in 1822, the subsequent problems and achievements in the technology of this science and industry have been virtually encyclopedic, especially so in the latter years of the nineteenth century. This thesis is not intended as a scientific investigation or critique of those machines and their inventors, but rather to give a brief, understandable description of the matrices and the patrices which were at the heart of all these devices. Many marvelous and ingenious ideas were proposed or put forth, often without reward for the now-forgotten inventors. The successful machines, as well as those which never saw practical use, have become part of the rich heritage of letterpress printing and are important milestones in the annals of American typographic invention. Some of these techniques and principles that were worked out in the nineteenth century pointed the way toward today's electronic/photographic technology, a reminder that there is nothing truly "new" under the sun. One can say of them, *requiescant in pace!*

POSTSCRIPT,
IN LIEU OF ACKNOWLEDGEMENTS

Sincere thanks is offered to the following people who have graciously supplied important information that helped to make this book possible: Richard L. Hopkins, printer, Terra Alta, West Virginia, who encouraged this project from the beginning and offered significant material on hand punchcutting; George Corban Goble, PhD, Berea, Kentucky, who supplied vital information on some of Mergenthaler's early work; Dr. James Eckman, Rochester, Minnesota, for his incisive remarks and information on various historical points; David Pankow, Rochester Institute of Technology, for his fine editorial work and literary guidance; Robert Fleck, Oak Knoll Books, New Castle, Delaware, who has given much encouragement, and taken on the onus of publishing this book. The help, criticism and suggestions of these people have contributed greatly to the historic and bibliographical value of this little-understood subject.

REFERENCES

1. Annenberg, Maurice, *Type Foundries of America and their Catalogs.* Baltimore: Maran Printing Services, 1975.

2. Bragdon, Charles R., *Metal Decorating From Start to Finishes.* Freeport, Maine: The Bond Wheelwright Company, 1961.

3. Brown, Oren L., *Brown's Patent Typesetting and Distributing Machinery.* Boston: Oren L. Brown, 1870.

4. Höhne, Otto, *Geschichte der Setzmaschinen.* Leipzig: Der Deutschen Buchdrucker G.M.B.H., 1925.

5. Huss, Richard E., *The Development of Printers' Mechanical Typesetting Methods, 1822–1925.* Charlottesville, Va.: University Press of Virginia, 1973.

6. Huss, Richard E., *Dr. Church's "Hoax."* Willow Street (sic), Pa., Graphic Crafts, Inc., 1976.

7. Legros, Lucien, and Grant, John C., *Typographical Printing-Surfaces.* London: Longmans, Green and Co., 1916.

8. Loy, William E., "Designers and Engravers of Type." Chicago: *The Inland Printer*, Vols. 20–25, 1897–1900.

9. MacKellar, Smiths & Jordan, *One Hundred Years, 1796–1896.* Philadelphia: MacKellar, Smiths & Jordan, 1896.

10. McArthur, Richard N., *The Book of OZ Cooper*, chapter "On Cooper Typefaces." Chicago: The Society of Typographic Arts, 1949.

11. Mengel, Willi, *Ottmar Mergenthaler and the Printing Revolution.* Brooklyn: Mergenthaler Linotype Co., 1954.

12. Mergenthaler Linotype Company, *Milestones of Machine Typesetting* Brooklyn: Mergenthaler Linotype Co., 1944.

13. Mergenthaler, Ott. & Company, *Catalogue A.* Baltimore: Ott. Mergenthaler & Co., (no printer), 1898.

14. Mergenthaler Printing Company, "Report of the Board of Directors, January 21, 1888." Original copy in Library of Congress. Information courtesy of Corban Goble.

15. Middleton, R. Hunter, *Making Printers' Typefaces.* Chicago: The Black Cat Press, 1938.

16. Middleton, R. Hunter, *An Essay on the Forgotten Art of the Punchcutter.* A talk on punch cutting, School of Library Service, University of California, Los Angeles, March 31, 1965.

17. Ringwalt, J. Luther, *American Encyclopaedia of Printing.* Philadelphia: Menemin & Ringwalt, 1871.

18. Sherman, Frank M., *The Genesis of Machine Typesetting.* Chicago: M & L Typesetting and Electrotyping Co., 1950.

19. Schoenrich, Carl Otto, *Biography of Ottmar Mergenthaler and History of the Linotype, Its Invention and Development.* Baltimore: The Friedenwald Company, 1898.

19.1 Seyl, Antoine, *La Composition Mécanique*. Bruxelles: Imprimerie Scientifique et Littéraire, 1926.

20. Thompson, John S., *History of Composing Machines*. Chicago: The Inland Printer Company, 1904.

21. A. Turpain, *The Development of Mechanical Composition in Printing*. Washington: Government Printing Office, 1908.

22. Yeaton, Charles C., *Manual of the Alden Type Setting and Distributing Machine*. New York: Francis Hart & Company, 1865.

INDEX

COLOPHON

Design by the author

Typesetting in Linotype "Janson," and printing letterpress by Heritage
    Printers, Charlotte, North Carolina 28202

Plates and linecuts by Ace Engraving Service, Ord, Nebraska 68862

Stamping die for cover by Cage Graphic Arts, Inc., Philadelphia, Pa. 19107

Plate section printed by Graphic Crafts, Inc., Willow Street, Pa. 17584

Binding by Hoster Bindery, Hatboro, Pa. 19040

The paper is Warren's Olde Style wove, substance 70.

This edition is limited to 400 copies.